AT
HOME
IN THE
MUDDY
WATER

*A Guide to Finding Peace
within Everyday Chaos*

Ezra Bayda

SHAMBHALA
Boston & London ∘ 2004

Shambhala Publications, Inc.
Horticultural Hall
300 Massachusetts Avenue
Boston, Massachusetts 02115
www.shambhala.com

9 8 7 6 5 4 3 2 1

FIRST PAPERBACK EDITION
Printed in the United States of America

This edition is printed on acid-free paper that meets the
American National Standards Institute z39.48 Standard.
Distributed in the United States by Random House, Inc.,
and in Canada by Random House of Canada Ltd

The Library of Congress catalogues the previous
edition of this work as follows:
Bayda, Ezra.
At home in the muddy water: a guide to finding peace
within everyday chaos
Ezra Bayda.
p. cm.
ISBN 1-59030-168-4 (paper)
ISBN 1-57062-947-1 (cloth)
1. Spiritual life—Zen Buddhism.
2. Compassion—Religious aspects—Buddhism. I. Title.
BQ9288 .B39 2003
294.3′444—dc21   2002013960

AT
HOME
IN THE
MUDDY
WATER

*All I can experience and work with
is what my life is right now. That's all I can do.
The rest is the dream of ego.*

—Charlotte Joko Beck

Contents

Contents

Acknowledgments

THIS BOOK IS A CONTINUATION of my first book, *Being Zen*. In a way, they make up one book; together the two present a particular approach to waking up from the self-centered dream we all live in.

I wish to acknowledge the same people I thanked in *Being Zen*—particularly my teacher, Joko Beck, for her clarity and precision; and also Stephen Levine and Pema Chödrön, for their emphasis on bringing practice to the heart.

Thanks to Carolyn Miller for the initial typing and editing of the manuscript; and to my daughter Jenessa for her thorough editing. The final editing was skillfully done by Emily Hilburn Sell, who did an excellent job clarifying what I was trying to say.

And last, I am continuously thankful to Elizabeth Hamilton, my wife, friend, and teacher, not only for her aspiration and keen intellect, but also for her irrepressible good cheer and wholehearted support.

Introduction

WHEN MY WIFE, ELIZABETH, and I were in Paris, we saw a large billboard in the subway station that read *Soyez Zen*. Literally, this means "Be Zen." It could be interpreted more generally as "Just Live" or "Appreciate the Sweetness of the Moment." Although the billboard was only an advertisement for futons, it made me realize how often we forget that practice is actually about *living*, about opening into *whatever* life presents. Isn't it true that we tend instead to equate spiritual practice with a particular technique, such as sitting in meditation, or with feeling a particular way, such as calm or centered?

Recently I gave a talk to a group of young adults, most in their twenties. I was amazed how easily they could articulate ideas about practice, such as the importance of letting life be, or of not trying to fix or change things. It was not that their stated views were inaccurate. What amazed me was that they discussed these things so casually, as if they could really live them. Yet making practice real is much more difficult than simple intellectual understanding. Anyone who has practiced for a while knows that the greatest barrier to waking up is that we don't realize how asleep we are. It takes more than reading books, hearing lectures, or meditating for a short while to understand how difficult practice really is.

If we don't begin to know ourselves, we cannot, as the saying goes, "see the way even as we walk on it." Knowing ourselves allows us to see what prevents us from opening into

Soyez Zen—just living. It allows us to see in what way and to what degree we are stuck in the mud, knee-deep in our galoshes.

During Zen meditation retreats, there's a verse that's recited after each meal:

> May we exist like a lotus
> At home in the muddy water.
> Thus we bow to life as it is.

What does it mean to be at home in the muddy water? What does it mean to bow to life as it is? The answers to these questions are what this book is about—clarifying the confusion of daily living, cultivating equanimity even within the high-speed messiness of life, and transforming our everyday suffering into the genuine life that all of us want. This entails knowing ourselves and all the ways we hold ourselves back in fear.

These things are not easy, but they *are* possible. My intent in writing this book is to communicate, as practically and specifically as possible, how to make the genuine life a lived reality. Using topics such as relationships, trust, sexuality, and money, the emphasis is on ways to become willing to "Soyez Zen," to *just be*, right in the middle of life. To do this, we must see the endless ways we keep ourselves stuck in the mud of our spinning minds, our habitual and protective patterns, and, of course, our fears.

If we decline this opportunity and continue to hold back in fear and protectedness, won't that bring about our deepest regret? We must take these words to heart, so that we can awaken to the basic kindness and connectedness that are the essential nature of our Being.

PART ONE

What Practice Is

I

What We're All Looking For

A Zen student walked in to see the master. Sitting down, he blurted out, "There's something terribly wrong with me!" The master looked at him and asked, "What's so wrong?" The student, after a moment's hesitation, responded, "I think I'm a dog." To that the master responded, "And how long have you thought that?" The student replied, "Ever since I was a puppy."

What does this story have to do with spiritual practice? Everything! It puts the basic human problem in a nutshell. The next time you find yourself immersed in the drama of a strong emotional reaction, awash with deeply believed thoughts, ask yourself how long you've taken these thoughts to be the truth. Especially notice the ones you believe the most: "Life is too hard." "No one will ever be there for me." "I'm worthless." "I'm hopeless." How long have you believed these thoughts? Ever since you were a puppy!

These deeply held beliefs may not be visible on the surface of our minds; we're often not even aware of them. Yet we cling to them because they've become rooted in our very cells—in our cellular memory. And their imprint on our lives is unmistakable. We engage in endless defensive strategies to avoid the pain of directly experiencing these beliefs and identities. These habitual coping patterns are our attempt to buffer us from the anxious quiver of insecurity, and to establish some sense of safety, security, and familiarity. They might include seeking achievements, becoming a helper, trying to control our world,

3

or withdrawing into safety. But do they ever give us a sense of genuine satisfaction? No. All too often they keep us stuck in dissatisfaction, not knowing where to turn. I call this stuck place "the substitute life."

If we're fortunate enough to aspire to become free of our substitute or artificial life, we may start questioning our most basic assumptions, including our very mode of living. Such questioning can be painful, but it's a prerequisite to leading a more genuine life. The one question that goes directly to the heart of the matter is: "What is my life really about?" Our honesty in answering this question will determine how clearly we understand the basic human predicament—that we are cut off from awareness of our own True Nature.

For example, how much of the day are you aware—just basically aware of what life is presenting—rather than being lost in waking sleep, in being identified with whatever you're doing, almost as if you didn't exist? Is a greater proportion of your time spent blindly drifting from one form of comfort to another, from one daydream or fantasy to another, from one safe place to another, in order to avoid the anxious quiver of discomfort or insecurity? How much of your energy is used to fortify a particular self-image, or to please others in order to gain approval, instead of devoting your energy to living a genuine life?

More specifically, can you see the particular ways in which you avoid really being with your life? Do you know what strategies you use to guarantee some sense of safety and familiarity, to avoid facing the fears—of rejection, loss, unworthiness, or failure—that lie beneath the surface of your thoughts and actions?

Do you, for example, try to maintain a sense of order and control, to avoid feeling the fear of chaos, of things falling apart? To avoid the fear of rejection, of not fitting in, do you try to gain acceptance and approval? How do you avoid the fear of feeling unworthy? By trying to excel and attain success? Do you seek busyness in adventure or pleasure, to avoid the deep holes of longing and loneliness? All of these strategies have one thing in common: they keep us encased in an artificial or substitute life.

None of us is beyond this. We all follow certain strategies to escape feeling the fears that silently run our life. Even when we know all about these fears, we don't usually want to have anything to do with them. Perhaps this sounds pessimistic and discouraging, but it doesn't have to be. In fact, it's only by realizing the extent to which we are asleep—how much we are driven by the vanity of our endeavors, the smallness of our attachments, and the urgency of avoiding our fears—that we can wake from our sleep, from our substitute way of living.

When we see that we're asleep, we might think we have to make superhuman efforts to wake up. We might look for technique after technique, or for more and more words of wisdom—but neither will give us the solution that we're looking for, especially if we fall into the trap of trying to fix or change ourselves. Genuine spiritual practice is never about fixing ourselves, because we're not broken. It's about becoming awake to who we really are, to the vastness of our True Nature, which includes even the parts of ourselves we label as "bad."

The essence of the practice life is cultivating awareness. This process has two basic aspects. The first is clarifying the mental process. The second is *experiencing*—entering into awareness of the physical reality of the present moment.

The practice of clarifying the mental process entails seeing through our substitute life; this means identifying our deeply believed thoughts and most basic identities. The point is to see that these beliefs and identities have become so solidified—as if it's *always* been this way—that we accept them as truth. We also have to see how our behavioral strategies, which always arise out of fear-based core beliefs, have become so conditioned that they, too, seem like the truth of our being.

As we see these thoughts and strategies clearly, we also have to deal with the emotional pain that originally gave rise to them—the pain that's embedded in our cellular memory. We do this through the process of *experiencing*. By bringing awareness to the physical sensations of the present moment, we can spark the transformation of our substitute life into a life that is more genuine. Paradoxically, this transformation happens only when we stop trying to change ourselves. In fact, trying to change is often the crux of the problem. We enter the process of experiencing not in order to change, but to leave the thought-based world and connect with the reality of what is. And as we enter this process, what actually happens?

Experiencing our lives transforms them because it eventually makes transparent the seeming solidity of our core beliefs. As we connect with the physical reality of the moment, we realize, experientially, that the apparent solidity of the self is actually a complex of deeply believed thoughts, habitual strategies, ancient memories, and sometimes unpleasant sensations. It's as if all our thoughts, judgments, emotions, and identities are separate aggregates, bound together into a solid world called "me." When we enter the present moment without concepts, we can *experience* that this apparently solid self is not exactly what it seems. As we stop identifying with the narrow sense of "me," we begin to identify with the wider container of awareness itself.

We can then experience the genuine life that we all intuitively seek—without which we will only experience dissatisfaction. This genuine quality can't be named—it's not an object. Yet it's more real than anything. It's who we really are. This is not something we can go looking for; it's already there. It will always elude us if we *try* to find it. But as we live the practice life and attempt to abide in whatever life presents, this quality is uncovered, appearing gradually, bit by bit, year by year.

The difficulty is that often we're not willing to be with whatever life presents to us. On the long path of awakening, as we dig deeper into ourselves and uncover layer after layer of falsehoods, we frequently just don't want to make the effort to practice. Sometimes this lack of effort can come from the simple desire to be comfortable. At other times, we simply can't go any deeper. There's only so much we can absorb before we feel the need to turn away. There's nothing wrong with this. In fact, it's perfectly understandable when we realize that what we're doing in practice is dismantling the notion of the self. This dismantling, where the solidity of the self becomes increasingly porous, has to proceed slowly for real transformation to occur. When we take in too much too soon, as many have done on drug trips or in sudden spiritual openings, the resulting insights are difficult to stably integrate into our being. Understanding that we can dig only so deep into the truth at any given time makes us less likely to fall into the trap of negative self-judgment when we see ourselves resisting practice.

A friend and fellow student told me about going to see Suzuki Roshi once in the late 1960s. My friend was feeling discouraged about his inability to practice consistently; he always seemed to be vacillating between effort and resistance, and he felt that there was something essentially wrong with his practice. Suzuki Roshi told him that this kind of vacillation was a universal issue in practice. Over and over, we try and try, and then we "fail." Then, at some point, we learn to go deeper.

Spiritual practice does not follow a straight line to a fixed goal; it's almost always a mixture of struggle and integration, of confusion and clarity, of discouragement and aspiration, of feeling failure and going deeper. Seeing through our deeply held beliefs, dismantling the solid sense of self, facing our worst fears, opening into the unknown—how could we even imagine that this wouldn't be a gradual and halting process, with many ups and downs? Coming to understand this means seeing through idealized pictures of how we're *supposed* to be and developing compassion for ourselves as we walk the path of awakening.

As we develop this sense of compassion, we are less likely to judge ourselves as "wrong" when we resist practice. Instead, we become more and more willing to let the resistance just be. Simply being with the ups and downs of life with less judgment is an essential step toward mature practice.

One of Suzuki's dharma successors, Kwong Roshi, who was my own teacher for fifteen years of traditional Zen practice, often stressed the importance of "learning to stand on our own two feet." This advice reminds me of the last words of Buddha, that we must learn to "be a lamp unto ourselves." Perhaps there is nothing more important in practice than understanding this advice properly; yet it's so easily regarded as a cliché or accepted only superficially, with no attempt to put it into practice.

The only way to understand what it means to be a lamp unto ourselves is to find our own lamp, which means enduring the long process of delving deeper and deeper into our being. It involves uncovering and seeing through layers and layers of conditioning embedded in our mind and body. Only when the depth and power of our deeply held beliefs and judgments become clear to us can we experience what it means to stand on our own two feet, to be a lamp unto ourselves. Only when we have the ability to stay with the painful dismantling of the solid sense of self can we awaken the heart that seeks to be awakened. The more we practice, the more our understanding deepens.

At every stage, we'll find a different answer to the question, "What is my life really about?" Even so, we have to ask this question again and again, lest we lose sight of the point of practice. It doesn't matter that for a long time the answer keeps changing, or that at times what we think is the answer is just the ego's wish for a life free from difficulty. Even though we don't know what our life is really about most of the time, we're still driven by our heart, which innately seeks to be awakened. To know that we don't know, yet to keep practicing, is the way we learn to go deeper.

Until we find the reality of life that we're all seeking, we'll continue to experience dissatisfaction. This reality can't be pinpointed with words, yet it's more genuine than anything we can speak of. All we can say is that it's *who we really are*. And to find out who we really are does not require that we seek an answer; rather, it calls on us to go deeper and deeper into uncovering the falsehoods of our substitute life, including our judgments, our identities, our deeply held beliefs. The Zen teacher Seng Ts'an said this clearly in his famous line: "Do not search for the truth; only cease to cherish opinions." To cease cherishing opinions—including no longer holding on to the core beliefs that define our identity as a solid, separate self—is the way we learn what it means to be a lamp unto ourselves.

The essential point is that we don't have to seek our True Nature or even any particular state of mind. Wherever you are, *whatever* your state of mind, can be the focus of your practice. Any distress you may feel—discomfort, anxiety, or emotional upset—is the path itself. It is the opportunity to awaken to a more genuine life. Our difficulties are always our best teachers—but only if we know how to learn from them. Seeing your mind clearly and experiencing yourself in the moment is how to unlock the door to a genuine life. In any given moment, you can ask yourself if you know what opinions you're holding onto. What happens to your body when you cling to them? What are you believing right now? What are you physically experiencing right now? You don't have to *do* anything except be aware.

The genuine life is rooted in a rock-bottom security that develops as we come to know who we really are. This security is based not on self-image or social conditions, but on a sense of strength, presence, and connection anchored in a growing awareness of the vastness of our True Nature.

2

Meditation as a
Transformative Process

I USED TO APPROACH SITTING MEDITATION, especially in practice retreats, with the idea that it was supposed to make me feel a special way. Often, I just wanted to be free from anxiety. As a result, however, I rarely had a clear idea of what sitting was really about. Even now that I'm no longer trying to get a special feeling from sitting, I still find it helpful to occasionally look at exactly what I'm doing in my sitting practice.

I find it particularly useful to revisit the basic questions: What is sitting really about? Why is it so important to sit? Why do we stress the necessity of daily sitting, as well as the necessity of the longer sittings in retreats? Obviously we don't sit just to feel good; often, especially at retreats, sitting doesn't feel good at all. We're sleepy, we ache, we're bored. We often don't remember why we're here. Sometimes we want nothing more than to leave. So why do we continue to sit? What are we doing? Do we know what is actually happening during sitting practice that makes it such a valuable process?

There are several interconnected components that make up the process of sitting. All of these components are essential aspects of meditation as a transformative process. Seeing the process clearly may help us to weather the inevitable low spots and dry spells. It will also help us redirect our practice when it begins to go off course. These components are neither sequential nor formulaic. At a given time, one of them may be more pertinent to your particular situation than the others.

The first factor is *perseverance*. Perseverance makes it possible to sit through discomfort, to sit when we don't feel like it, to sit when we're bored or tired. It makes it possible to stay with practice through all of the valleys, the low spots, the difficulties. Perseverance is no small thing, because at times our resistance can be very strong. Isn't it a fact that we often don't want to stay with the experience of the present moment for more than a few seconds? So cultivating perseverance over the years is like building a muscle; we develop the strength and capacity without which practice could never really develop. Basically, we learn that practice doesn't have to please us in the ordinary sense for us to continue practicing.

The second factor is the process of *settling down*. Picture a clear glass of water with a layer of mud at the bottom. Imagine stirring up the water so that it becomes muddy. This muddy water is our substitute life—swirling with anxiety and confusion. We race around trying to keep up, but with little clarity about what we're doing. Taking this glass and setting it down is like setting ourselves down to sit. What happens? In the glass, the mud gradually settles to the bottom, and the water becomes clear and still. In sitting, we learn what it feels like to settle down. This settling happens over the years on both a psychological and a physical level. There is something strengthening about not moving when the impulse to move arises in us. Instead, we just stay still, not feeding the agitation, not stirring up the water anymore. It is here that we might use a concentration technique, such as focusing on the breath, to help us settle. Granted, this settling and clarity do not always happen; sometimes as we sit even more mud—from our subterranean internal world—comes rising to the surface. Yet, over time, sitting fosters a settled quality, an equanimity, in the midst of the muddy turmoil of our lives.

This quality is well expressed in the line that is frequently recited at Zen temples:

> May we exist like a lotus
> At home in the muddy water.

The third factor is *clear seeing*. This is the process of observing everything we do—how we think, what we think, how we react, what our strategies are, how they emerge from our core beliefs—and how they all tie together into a defensive, apparently solid "substitute life."

Clear seeing is not the same as psychoanalyzing; we're *not* focusing on the past or trying to figure out why we think or behave as we do. This is an important point. We're simply attempting to observe ourselves as we are. As we begin seeing through our beliefs and strategies, we inevitably judge and find fault with ourselves. But part of the practice of clear seeing is to observe our mind's tendency to judge and to notice how often we're not even aware of accepting our judgments as truth.

Clear seeing of our basic belief systems begins to undermine our deep-seated conditioning. Our conditioning doesn't disappear, but it no longer runs our life. Clear seeing is like taking off filtered glasses; reality becomes sharper, more distinct. We don't need to struggle to change our behavior; clear seeing broadens our perspective to embrace new possibilities of behavior. Change comes as a natural consequence of this.

The practice of *thought labeling* plays an important part in this process. Unless we label our thoughts as we see them, we'll most likely continue to believe them. Thought labeling involves repeating to ourselves whatever thought crosses our mind: "Having a believed thought that life isn't fair," or "Having a believed thought that nothing ever works out." We label almost as if there were a parrot on our shoulder. Doing this breaks our identification with the thoughts we have; it removes our investment in them. Moreover, we see, very precisely, what it is we believe. Labeling the specific thoughts allows us to begin to see our thoughts *as* thoughts. We don't label every thought; otherwise our meditation would become too mental. But *whenever* we feel emotional tension, we use that as a signal that there's some belief system in place that we don't see clearly. As we begin to see these beliefs with clarity, and as we no longer identify with these beliefs as who we are, we can move out of the narrow mental tunnel of our substitute life. Thus the basic human problem—the fabrication and perpetuation of a "me," based in fear and protectedness—becomes clarified.

When I started my first meditation group, there were about twenty people who came regularly, meeting in my small apartment. As low-key as this may sound, it still triggered some anxiety in me. Labeling my believed thoughts allowed me to see that I was living out of two separate pictures. The first picture was the negative core belief "I can't do this!" The second picture was a strategy to cope with that core belief, "I have to be smart, calm, and together." This new and challenging situation made it very clear that my whole life I had ping-ponged back and forth between these two pictures, believing whichever one was dominant as the only truth. Both pictures were, of course, born of the same unhealed pain—the anxious quiver of our basic sense of unworthiness.

Seeing through these beliefs helped me to realize that I no longer had to struggle with my anxiety in the ordinary sense, which always entails trying to change it or get rid of it in some way. In clearly *seeing*, my conditioned beliefs became increasingly obvious and familiar. Seeing them and labeling them again and again allowed a lightness of heart to gradually replace the usual self-judgment. And with the beliefs and judgments defused, I was left with just the bodily experience of anxiety itself.

This leads to the fourth aspect of sitting practice—*experiencing our emotional distress*. Although this is one of the most difficult aspects of practice, it is also the path of accelerated transformation—where the energy of our emotions is transformed through the process of experiencing them. For example, when I felt anxiety about teaching my first students and saw my conditioned beliefs clearly, all I had to do was open to the anxiety, to reside in it, to rest in it. It wasn't necessary to judge the distress or push it away, but just to *experience* what it was. We rarely allow ourselves to do this. Mostly we fuel emotional distress by believing our thoughts and stringing them together into a story line, which we then rehash. Once we've learned to label thoughts and clarify the mental process, we can focus instead on the physical texture of our experience.

Sometimes, when emotions are particularly intense, such as in hurt or grief or overwhelment, it's very difficult to prac- tice because the feelings of groundlessness and helplessness are so uncomfortable. But this is also the very place where we can enter into the heart of practice, where we can begin to break through the layers of armoring and protection we've all erected to feel more secure. In erecting this armoring, particu- larly in holding onto our self-images, our pretenses, our pro- tective identities, we've cut ourselves off from our hearts. And in talking about our hearts, I'm not talking about the physical muscle, or some vague pseudospiritual idea; I'm talk- ing about the Heart that is the essential nature of our Being. In some traditions this Heart is called Emptiness; in other tra- ditions it's called God. But it doesn't matter what words we use—this Heart is the Heart that only knows connectedness and love.

In working with intense emotions, we have the opportunity to break through our protective cocoon, and thereby enter into the spaciousness of the Heart. But because it is so difficult to stay with these emotions, this process is best done within the wider container and stillness of meditation, a process that al- ways entails awareness of the physical experience of the pres- ent moment.

A particularly valuable tool is to ask the question or koan, "What *is* this?" This is called a koan in Zen because it can't be answered with the mind. Practicing with this question takes us away from analysis and thinking, back into the immediate sensory quality, the *whatness*, of our experience. As with all koans, the answer to this question can never be conceptual. It's not what the emotion is *about*—it's what it *is*. In fact, the only answer is our immediate experience itself. Asking "What *is* this?" reminds us to focus our attention like a laser beam on that place we rarely want to visit—the discomfort of our immediate experience. Bringing our attention to the physical reality of the moment means, in part, focusing on specific sensations in the body. Is there tension? Where? What does it feel like? When we bring our attention to this unwanted place and stay with it, our emotional distress loses its solidity.

At this point it's equally important to bring kindness to our practice. This means abandoning our hard-hearted judgments about ourselves. When we come to meditation with the mistaken belief that meditation is supposed to make us feel good, we will no doubt fall into the unkindness of our self-judgment as difficulties inevitably arise. But in bringing the curiosity of "what *is* this?" mind to our experience, we are engendering the essential ingredient of willingness. Isn't it the willingness to just be with *whatever* arises that brings the element of kindness to our practice? With the heartfelt touch of a willing awareness, we begin to rest in a sense of spaciousness and lightness. When we really *experience* in this way, it's like taking off a pair of tight shoes. The sense of restriction and limitation dissolves. This is how the practice of experiencing emotional distress transforms us.

The last aspect is bringing our attention to *just this moment.* We always have the choice either to spin off into thinking or to just be here, with whatever the moment brings. This choice point is the basis of our sitting practice, in which we notice our particular patterns of inattention to the present moment. Do we habitually spin off into planning, fantasizing, self-judging? Do we tend to dwell in reliving the past or imagining the future? In noticing our patterns and returning to the present, we make the choice moment after moment to just be here. Doing this, we develop the awareness that allows thoughts and emotions to pass through us without our getting "hooked."

One technique that many have found helpful in developing this wider container of awareness is called *dual awareness* practice. In dual awareness, you maintain simultaneous attention on the specific sensations of the breath and the specific perceptions of sound. This is more than a concentration practice, because you're not focused exclusively on these two components of awareness. You bring roughly a third of your attention to the breath and sounds. The rest of your awareness is open to experiencing any other sensations or perceptions that arise.

Try this now: Bring your awareness to the specific sensations of the breath. Feel the coolness of the breath as it enters your nostrils, and then feel the subtle texture in the nose as you exhale. Feel the sensations in the chest and shoulders as they rise and fall with each inhalation and exhalation. Experience the feelings of expansion and contraction in the belly as the breath comes in and goes out. Now feel all of these sensations together—on the inbreath, the coolness in the nostrils, the rising of the upper body, and the expansion of the belly; and on the outbreath, the subtle texture in the nose, the falling of the upper body, and the contraction in the belly. Stay with these physical sensations for a few cycles of the breath. Then expand the awareness to include the perception of sounds. Include not only the varied ambient sounds, but also the sounds between the sounds, the sounds of silence. Staying with this dual experience of breath and sounds, widen the awareness so that the experience of breathing and listening take up only about one-third of your attention. Allow any other sensations and perceptions to come into awareness, feeling them within the wider container of breathing and listening.

Because one aspect (breath) is "inner" and the other (sound) is "outer," this practice takes us out of our normal myopic focus on "me," with all its attendant judgments and opinions. This is where we can experience the equanimity of just being. Equanimity is simply the willingness to be with whatever our life is, minus our judgments about it, minus our need to struggle to change it. This is not a passive kind of resignation. Dual awareness is very alert, very present; but it's a presence that can experience life as it is without feeling the need to fix it.

All of these factors—perseverance, letting the body and mind settle through stillness, clearly seeing our belief systems, experiencing our emotional distress, and just being with the moment—are part of the transformative process that allows us to be with and appreciate our life as it is. As we deepen this ability, we can experience the essential connectedness that is the nature of our Being. This is why we practice—to come to know the truth of who we really are. Yet we can't experience this truth, this basic connectedness, simply because we want to. We have to work with and understand the basic process of sitting.

How can knowing about these factors actually help us during sitting? When we've trained ourselves to ask that most basic practice question—"What is going on right now?"—what we'll usually see is that we're spaced out, lost in fantasy or planning, or caught in some kind of emotional distress. At that point we can ask the second basic practice question: "What is practice in this situation?"

Knowing that there are five things we could do—persevere, settle down, clarify our beliefs, experience the emotion, or just be—allows us to see more clearly what we need to do. This is not a precise formula. We don't sit there and analyze what we need to do. The effort involved is more subtle, closer to art than to science. But the art of sitting still requires the kind of understanding that allows us to know how to direct our efforts. For example, if we're caught in a low spot, feeling unmotivated or dry, we might simply stay and persevere. If we're caught in busy mind, with the familiar sense of agitation in the body, we remember to allow the body-mind to settle. If we're feeling emotional distress, we look at our unlabeled beliefs, see them clearly without self-judgment, then reside in the physical experience of discomfort. And if we're simply sitting, we know the subtle soft effort that is required to keep us in the moment.

Just knowing the process of transformation on an intellectual level, without having done the work, won't help at all. On the other hand, doing the work without the understanding makes the work that much harder. Understanding what we're doing is often de-emphasized in Zen practice. But for the mind that prefers to operate on more than faith alone, having this knowledge of meditation as a transformative process is not only useful, it's essential.

3
The Measure of Practice

ON THE FIRST DAY of a four-day meditation retreat, a student went in to see the Zen master with whom he'd been studying for many years. Sitting at the teacher's feet, he asked, "Can you tell me how I'm doing in my practice?" The Zen master thought for a minute, then said, "Open your mouth." The student opened his mouth and the teacher peered in and said, "Okay, now bend your head down." The student bent his head down and the Zen master looked into his hair, then said, "Okay, now open your eyes really wide." The student opened his eyes and the Zen master glared into them and said, "You're doing fine." Then he rang his bell.

Because the teacher rang his bell, the student had to leave. The next day he returned, quite perplexed by what had happened the day before. "I asked you how I was doing in my practice yesterday, and you made me open my mouth, bend my head, and open my eyes. What did all that have to do with my practice?" The Zen master bowed his head in thought. Then he said, "You know, you're not really doing very well in your practice, and the truth is, I am not sure you are ever going to make it." Again he rang his bell.

The student walked out. You can imagine how confused and angry he felt. The next day he went back, still fuming, and said, "What do you mean, I'm not going to make it in practice? Do you know that I sit in meditation for an hour every day? Sometimes I sit twice a day. I come to every retreat. I have really deep experiences. What do you mean I'm not going to make it?" Again the master just sat there, apparently thinking. Then he said, "Well, maybe I made a mistake. Perhaps you're doing pretty well after all." And again he rang his bell.

There was one more day in the retreat. The student went back to see his teacher, utterly exhausted. He felt distraught and confused, but he was no longer fighting it. He said to the master, "I just wanted to know how I was doing in my practice." This time the teacher looked at him and with no hesitation, in a very kind voice, said, "If you really want to know how you're doing in your practice, just look at all of your reactions over the last few days. Just look at your life."

It's important to have a daily meditation practice, to have a developing ability to see thoughts clearly, and to reside in our bodily experience. But having deep experiences during meditation is not enough. If we want to know how we're doing in our practice, we have to look at our life. Unless we begin to connect it with the rest of our life, our practice—however strong, calm, or enjoyable—ultimately will not be satisfying.

The reason it won't be satisfying is that we're ignoring one of the three basic pillars of practice. The first pillar is a daily sitting practice, in which we slowly develop both the strength and the willingness to do what we've spent our whole lives avoiding: reside in the physical reality of the present moment. The second pillar is the more intensive training offered in retreats, which pushes us in a way that we would rarely push ourselves at home. There is no substitute for the learning we can do at retreats—where our illusions are dismantled and the real value of perseverance becomes clear. The third pillar is practicing with the messy, unromantic, ordinary ups and downs of our everyday life. This pillar is essential to a genuine practice life. Without it, we will never truly be satisfied.

However, understanding the connection between practice and the rest of our life means addressing many different concerns. For instance, how are you practicing in your relationships—with your spouse, your children, your parents, with people at work? How many resentments do you still hold on to? Do the same people as ever in your life trigger anger, contempt, or other believed judgments? To what extent can you say, "I'm sorry," and really mean it?

How are you practicing at work? How many of your particular job requirements do you believe *must* be met? When a problem arises, can you say "yes" to practicing with it, even when you hate what's happening? And when criticism comes at you, are you willing to work with your reactions when they arise, instead of justifying them?

Are you becoming aware of your most deeply held beliefs, and how through your behavioral strategies they run the whole show? Is the sense of drama or emergency that arises around your emotional conflicts any lighter? Are you any more willing to open to your core pain, to soften your armoring and protection? Do you experience appreciation, satisfaction, humor, or quiet joy—at least occasionally?

The answers to questions like these give us the measure of our practice. This measure is nothing magical or mysterious. It's simply the increasing ability to know what our life is, as well as the growing understanding that to practice with our life means to practice with *everything* we meet. Practice isn't just about sitting on a cushion trying to feel calm.

It is not at all uncommon for students to ask their teacher to measure their practice for them. The question itself, if we're not aware of what we're really asking, is already one small measure of where we are. Needing to ask "How am I doing in my practice?" is like asking "Am I okay?" or "Am I acceptable the way I am?"

A friend recently told me that she learned three things about herself in assessing her practice: she was addicted to her thinking, she was attached to her emotions, and she didn't want to stay in the present moment for more than a few seconds at a time. This might sound like familiar bad news, but is there really any problem with this? At least there's awareness of where we're stuck. What's unfortunate is *believing* our judgments and discouraging thoughts about what we see—"I'm a bad student," "I'll never really change," and so on.

We all want to change, to make our lives better. But most transformative changes are slow and almost imperceptible. Yet we continue to believe that our lives should be significantly different after practicing for only a few years. But it's not as if we go in to see a teacher, full of our fears, and come out fearless! Nor can we go to a retreat full of confusion, have a deep experience, and then remain permanently clear! We would like to see dramatic changes, but this isn't how practice works. Sometimes we don't even notice the ways it erodes our habitual protective strategies, until one day we find ourselves in a situation that had always made us anxious or angry or uptight, and we notice that the anxiety, the anger, or the closed-down quality is gone.

Rather than "How am I doing?" the real questions are "Where am I still shutting down in fear and self-protection?" and "Where do I meet my edge, beyond which I'm not ready to go?" Practice is about noticing and experiencing these places— not with heaviness or guilt, but just as stuff to be worked with—and then seeing how to take small steps beyond them.

For example, when faced with a difficult decision and lost in confusion, are we able to see clearly how to practice? Students often ask for help when trying to decide whether to stay in a relationship or make a career change. They're often caught in the mental snare of weighing and measuring the pros and cons of each position, spinning among possibilities with no hope of resolution. But confusion is a state out of which nothing but confusion arises; the real source of confusion in such situations is that we don't know who we are. As the French philosopher Pascal said, "The heart has reasons of which the mind knows nothing."

To practice with difficult decisions, we must leave the mental world and enter the heart of our experience. This means residing in the physical experience of the anxiety and confusion itself, instead of spinning off into thoughts. How does it actually feel to be confused? What is the texture of the experience? Staying with the bodily reality of the present moment offers us the possibility to see our life with a clarity that we could never realize through thinking alone. How long will it take? No one can say. But practicing like this is a good example of going to our edge and working directly with where we're stuck.

Another example of practicing at our edge is in working with addiction. We all have addictions—behaviors to which we keep returning because they promise pleasure, though they ultimately deliver only dissatisfaction. Where do your addictions lie: with food, sex, approval, work? No matter what form our addictive pattern takes, when we find ourselves at that edge where we just can't refrain from the behavior, we can practice by discontinuing one small aspect of the behavior. The idea here isn't to wipe out the addiction, but to truly *experience* the energy behind the behavior, the seemingly unquenchable thirst from which addictive behaviors arise.

For example, if you're addicted to eating for comfort, you could practice not eating snacks at night for a week. The goal is not to never eat snacks again or to become a spiritual ascetic. Rather, the idea is that for just one week you give yourself the opportunity to work with the hole of discomfort out of which your craving arises. The practice is to refrain in order to take yourself to the edge of the longing and work with it.

Another example is working with your fears. What do you do with your fears when they arise? Do you usually vacillate between trying to stomp them out and trying to avoid the fearful situation? Most of us do. But when we come to our edge—and what is fear if not the clearest indicator that we're at our edge—we can take the small practice step of choosing to go against our habitual reactions to fear. This is *not* done with the intention of modifying our behavior by stomping out our fear. Instead, we take the moment to observe and experience as fully as possible what our fear really is. The next time fear arises, see if you can really feel the energy of fear in the body, without doing anything to change it or get rid of it.

Practice always involves seeing our edge and taking a small step beyond it into the unknown. As a Spanish proverb says, "If you do not dare, you do not live." Nietzsche echoed this when he said, "The secret of the greatest fruitfulness and the greatest enjoyment of existence is: to live dangerously!" Nietzsche wasn't necessarily talking about doing physically dangerous things; he meant taking a step beyond our edge of comfort.

This edge marks a unique measure of practice for each of us, because what seems easy for one person is another's greatest fear. Seeing that others get stuck where we don't, and vice versa, makes everything seem a little more workable. Working with our edge also helps us develop more compassion for ourselves because as we practice going beyond it, we're no longer so quick to judge ourselves as hopeless when we can't.

Still, we have to step toward our edge by ourselves. Instead of regarding our edge as an enemy, a place we prefer to avoid, we can realize that our edge is actually *our path*. From this place we can take step closer toward what *is*. But we can only do this one step at a time, persevering through all the ups and downs of our lives. We may sense danger; sometimes we may even feel as if death is upon us. However, we don't have to leap in head first, going for all or nothing. We can simply take a small step, supported by the knowledge that everyone feels fear in stepping beyond the illusion of comfort.

The real measure of practice is whether, little by little, we can find our edge, that place where we're closed down in fear, and allow ourselves to experience it. This takes courage, but courage isn't about becoming fearless. Courage is the willingness to experience our fears. And as we experience our fears, courage grows. Noticing our edge and trying to meet it also allows us to develop compassion, not just for ourselves, but for the whole human drama. Then, with an increasing sense of lightness and curiosity, we can keep moving toward a more open and genuine life.

4
Potato Salad

EVERYTHING WE OBSERVE is in some way related to something else, which in turn is related to something else again. In other words, each element of our life is part of a system, and each system is a part of another system. No single theory can ever really explain or even describe the complexity of this interrelatedness, nor can it take into account the subjective filter of the person explaining. Yet we constantly try to figure out our world by categorizing, simplifying, and generalizing.

Furthermore, we think we can experience this world only through our perceptions. But as filtered pictures of a perceived reality, our perceptions are never accurate. We think we see reality, we think we sometimes even know reality, but what we see is our own bubble of perception, filtered through the mental constructs of time, space, and causality, as well as our associations, desires, language, and conditioning. We don't see things as *they* are, we see them as *we* are.

On the day-to-day level, when what we perceive fails to match our ideas of how things should be, we experience emotional and physical distress. When what we experience is contrary to what we want—and what we want almost always involves being free from discomfort and pain—we experience suffering.

Suppose, for example, that I expect my mate to protect me. What happens when my mate doesn't protect me? In fact, what happens when my mate not only doesn't protect me, but criticizes me instead? Most likely, I'll experience some form of distress—an emotional and bodily reaction that won't feel good. Reactions like this are frequently based on unfulfilled expectations, rooted in clouded perceptions and simplistic notions of others, ourselves, and human relationships.

Even though we know we're living in a complex world of interconnections, we tend to focus on just one element of any given situation: Why is this happening to me? Who can I blame? How can I fix it? With a subtle arrogance, we reduce the web of interrelationships to a simplified version of an answer we can never really know. We could just as arbitrarily attribute our distress to the potato salad we ate for lunch.

When life isn't going as we wish, practice is neither to seek explanations nor to assign blame. We can practice simply being with the "what" on as many levels as we can, rather than looking for the "why." Once again we ask the koan, "What *is* this?" The answer to this question is always our experience itself—residing in, being present to, our experience itself. This "what" *is* the present moment. And this is where real understanding lies: not in the mental world of "why," not in intellectual description, but in experiencing directly the ambiguous perceptual complexity of the present moment.

Try this now: Sit down in an erect but relaxed posture. Try to sit without moving around. Take a couple of deep breaths to bring your awareness to the body. Specifically, feel any sensations in the chest and belly area. Ask yourself, "What *is* this moment?" To answer, don't think about it; just feel the energy, the vibration there. If there is any discomfort, don't try to avoid it or change it; instead, feel the quality of the experience. When your mind wanders away, and it will, simply come back to the torso, asking again, "What *is* this moment?" Go deeper, really feeling the energy and texture of the moment. Stay with the experience in the body, feel it. Stay there. Breathe. Hear the sounds. Feel the air around you. Just sitting there, feel your own presence. And just stay with that.

This exercise was very short, but perhaps you got a taste of the fact that there are no words that can ever capture the quality or texture of the visceral experience of the present moment. But there's an aliveness to the present moment; there's a sense of freedom when we can willingly let our experience just be. By staying in the present moment, which is the doorway into reality, we can ultimately find a satisfaction and an equanimity that are not available in a life based mainly on thinking or in struggling to fix and control our world.

Gutei was a Zen master who lived sometime during the ninth century. Whenever students would come to see him, he would always respond in the same way, no matter what their question or dilemma. He would simply raise his index finger, saying nothing. With that, the interview would end.

Can you imagine going to see a teacher time and again, presenting your well-considered question or quandary, and getting only silence in return? Gutei was reflecting the student's experience right back to the student. The student would be forced to experience the frustration of not getting an answer, not getting intellectual clarity or psychological insight, not hearing about "why." Instead, he would have to return to the "what" of his experience.

As we practice experiencing this "what" with fewer filters, our self-imposed boundaries dissolve, and the bubble of perception of our separate self can burst, even if only momentarily. This is far different from striving to have "enlightenment experiences," through which we hope to achieve a permanent state of clarity and calm. This is a false pursuit; no single experience makes us permanently clear and peaceful. In fact, the pursuit of this fantasy state is often driven by the very same greed and ambition we are trying to dispel. Instead, I'm talking about the slow experiential dismantling of layer after layer of our illusions about who we are and what our life is. *Experiencing*, rather than trying to have special experiences, is where real freedom lies. This is how we learn that our normal way of looking at the world is only a description, and only one of many possible descriptions.

Nietzsche said that every word is a preconceived judgment. Consider the word *ego*. Using the word *ego* leads us to view it as an independent thing. But "ego" is just a concept describing a cluster of preconceived judgments that is definitely not one entity. This is an example of how ideas can limit us, imprison us. This individual "self" is just an idea, nothing more. To see through words and ideas is to come closer to knowing who we really are, and to understanding what life is truly about.

When problems arise in our life, we usually want simple answers: yes or no, this or that. But reality is a world of subtlety and paradox, a world of complexity, continuums, and change. We want to know why (why is this happening?) and how (how can I fix it?). We want the feeling of perceived comfort that comes when we think we've finally figured life out. But the truth is, we'll never figure life out. We'd be better off chalking it up to the potato salad and simply residing in the "what." Residing in the experiential "what" is the way we find the rock-bottom security that is possible from practice.

The reason we'll never figure life out by asking "why" and "how" is that it's impossible to say what life is. In fact, *life isn't anything*. It's not meaningful, it's not meaningless, it's not a challenge, it's not an opportunity, it's not a process, it's not a nonduality. Life isn't difficult or hopeless. Nor does it correspond to any of the other colorings of mind we use to describe and explain what we think and feel. *Life is what it is.* And even saying *that* isn't saying anything!

Nevertheless, we continue to believe in our thoughts, especially those most deeply conditioned. It's our urgent need to avoid the groundlessness, the anxious quiver of being, that drives us to embrace our concepts, our beliefs, our judgments—in order to gain some footing, a measure of security, a sense of living in a known world. And, of course, there's the juicy gratification of "being right."

What are we really doing when, for example, we sit in meditation allowing ourselves to get lost in planning? We're simply living in the mental world, where we can try to make life ordered, stable, and predictable. We're avoiding the "whatness"—the discomfort and uncertainty of the present moment. In those moments when we fall into the muddy water of uncertainty, can we just stay with the "what" of our experience without escaping into thinking, analyzing, judging, blaming, or believing?

Staying in the "what" has nothing to do with wallowing. Wallowing involves *believing* in our thoughts and opinions. To stay in the "what" is to experience the moment with all of its uncertainty—without the ground of thoughts and concepts, with no knowledge of what is to come. This is just the place where we least want to be.

But as long as we continue to push the truth of the moment away—whether by attempting to figure it out or through flights into our comfortable addictions and fantasies—the heaviness, drama, distress and dis-ease of our life will persist. As we insist on believing in our thoughts and judgments, we will continue to shut ourselves off from the depth, the genuineness, and the satisfaction available to all of us in every moment.

5
The Dry Spot

THE VERY FIRST TIME I sat in formal meditation, I had the distinct and eerie sensation that my body had disappeared. Though I'd never sat before, I'd received good instructions before the forty-minute sitting, and I tried very hard to stay focused. I can't say I didn't have expectations; I at least had the expectation that meditation would help me become calm. But I certainly didn't expect to feel that my body disappeared! When I told the sitting instructor about it, he called what I'd experienced a "free ride." He said that many people sit for ten or twenty years hoping for just such an experience. I remember wondering why anyone would want to feel like that.

I later learned about free rides, those new and interesting states of mind that seem to come so easily in the beginning stages of practice. But when I was in the middle of this honeymoon stage—where everything seems so fresh, so mysterious, so juicy—I simply took these exciting highs to be a natural part of the process. As the honeymoon wore thin, however, as disappointment upon disappointment set in, as practice uncovered my projections and illusions, my experience of practice became more dry.

The "dry spot" can be an acute, dramatic, and short-term condition or a subtle, chronic, long-term process. In either case, when we hit the dry spot, not only is the honeymoon over, but we also have little connection with the aspiration that originally brought us to practice. We've lost contact with that "still small voice within" that seeks to be awakened.

The short-term dry spot is often the result of unfulfilled expectations about practice. It isn't bringing us the immediate peace, calm, or freedom from fear that we had hoped for. Disappointment often leads to anger, and anger leads to resistance. When it becomes clear that neither the practice nor the teacher will save us, we blame the practice for being inadequate or the teacher for being flawed. Negative projections replace our pretty pictures. We lose touch with our aspiration, choosing instead to stew in our negative thoughts and opinions about practice.

It's important to understand that there's nothing wrong with the process of vacillating between aspiration and resistance. The dry spot is one particular and predictable manifestation of this natural cycle. But the first few times it hits us, it doesn't seem natural at all. The perceptions that arise seem like permanent truths about reality, rather than believed thoughts based on the changing cycles of a process.

My own early experiences with the dry spot followed an almost classic pattern. When I joined my first group, a Gurdjieff community, I was zealous in trying to know everything I could about practice and in wanting to do everything "the right way." The only problem with this approach was that I actually began to believe that I knew a lot. In fact, after about three years I thought I knew more than the teacher! Having placed him on a pedestal for the first couple of years, I began to see what I thought were his faults. First I believed my projection of who I wanted him to be and what I wanted him to do for me, and then I felt disappointment that he didn't fulfill my projection.

Feeling the disappointment of seeing through my illusions was a good thing. The problem was that I replaced one illusion with another. When my expectations were disappointed, I replaced them with negative thoughts about the teacher, thoughts that I believed without question. Because I didn't see that my unfulfilled expectations were the source of my disappointment,

I felt justified in blaming it on the teacher. No doubt some of my observations about the teacher were objectively accurate, but that was beside the point. Rather than focus on my own experience, I scrutinized what I saw as the teacher's faults. As a result, my aspiration began to dry up; solidified negative views took its place, leading me to temporarily leave the group. Gradually I saw through what I was doing and was able to return with renewed aspiration.

Several years later, when I decided to move from the Gurdjieff practice to a traditional Zen practice, I was aware of the tendency to project expectation onto the teacher. I wasn't aware, however, that we can do the same thing with the practice itself. I became a Zen student with the hazy, somewhat idealized notion that if I practiced hard and long enough, I'd be free from anxiety and fear. Since this isn't exactly how practice works, after several years of trying hard I began to lose my motivation. Although I didn't have a problem with the teacher, I gradually became less enchanted with the ability of practice to fulfill my personal agendas.

During one period my disappointment became so acute that even though I held a prominent position in the Zen community, I could barely tolerate being there. I resigned from my position and stopped going to retreats. Knowing that to leave the group entirely would be a mistake, I forced myself to go for just one meditation period a week. It was as if I were hanging on by a thread, and the thread was the difficult effort of just showing up. I had no interest in meditating, and I hated being there. Even though I continued to stay connected, the connection felt almost dead. I was caught in my blind and negative beliefs about practice; which arose directly from my unfulfilled agenda to get the goodies that were supposed to come with practicing hard.

Fortunately for me, I was able to wait out this dry period of bitter disappointment and gradually reenter the practice with a renewed and deepened sense of aspiration. There was no one dramatic moment where I saw the light; I just slowly saw through my doubt and negativity.

Often students leave practice when they hit a dry spot. But if we're fortunate and can wait it out, we begin to understand these natural cycles of resistance. We can even come to expect the doubting mind to arise. But doubting in itself is not the problem. The problem comes from believing the doubting thoughts and, more so, from identifying with this doubting "me," as who we are. Doubt can lead to a deepening in our quest, but only when we don't get lost in the negative beliefs that arise with that doubt.

As practice takes hold and we learn to cut through our story line, we can learn how to use doubt and distress as an opportunity to go deeper and experience the grief of our unfulfilled dreams. We can learn to rest in, to reside in, the *physical* experience of doubt itself, instead of following the line of negative thoughts. This can be difficult; the thoughts seem so true, so solid, so compelling. But as we rest in the doubt, even as the anguish of not knowing remains, the dryness can be transfused with a deeper sense of aspiration. Thomas Merton expressed this clearly: "True love and prayer are learned in the moment when prayer has become impossible and the heart has turned to stone." He's talking about the process of surrender. But surrender isn't something we can force. Yet, when we understand the cycles of resistance and can wait out a dry period by resting in the physical reality of doubt and distress, we will gradually feel a sense of renewal and direction.

The longer, more chronic dry spot is more subtle, and consequently more difficult to practice with. We may not even see it. At such a time, we'll usually continue, and even become good at, the outer forms of practice. We will also become comfortable with our level of attainment in the practice; we may even become confident in our ability to understand and communicate practice ideas. But in this more subtle dry spot, we might get just a little *too* comfortable. Perhaps some self-importance creeps in to replace what was once our beginner's mind; we become "senior students" and perhaps even aspiring teachers. Our practice may not even seem dry. But as we become more secure and comfortable in the practice, we move further away from what practice is really about.

During a long-term dry spell, the chances are good that we're using practice, at least in part, as a protective cover. These are questions we can ask ourselves to blow that cover: Are we using practice to feel the security of being part of a group. Do we use it to maintain the identity of a "Zen student," or a "spiritual seeker"? Are we seeking the comfort of following the practice in the "right" way?

In using practice as a cover, we're avoiding the groundlessness, the core pain, the anxious quiver of being that underlies all of our protections. Because we're no longer feeling the truth of our situation, practice slowly dries up, becoming lifeless and stagnant. We often don't want to even look at what's happening, because underneath it lies the fear that without our protective identities and props we would be no one. Perhaps a part of us knows that we're avoiding what we really need to do; but when we get the occasional glimpse of fear, we push it back out of awareness. Consequently, the dry spot just gets drier.

What is the solution to long-term, subtle dryness in practice? Perhaps we need a radical shake-up. Perhaps we even need to leave practice as we know it. By "as we know it," I mean the way we use practice as a cover or to run our habitual coping strategies, whether it be to hide (a favorite of Zen students), to be on top, to be compliant or dutiful, or even to be confused. Each of these strategies is useful in maintaining the security of our familiar self. Looking honestly at how we're using practice as a defensive strategy can shake us out of the chronic dry periods.

To leave practice as we know it may mean taking a step toward our edge, toward the discomfort of the unfamiliar. We have to look at how we're desperately trying to avoid all the things we know we eventually have to face. Once we see our strategy, whether it be to please, to win, or to hide in a self-image, we know perhaps we'll have to go against it. We might have to give up our cover identity—whatever it takes to shake us out of our sense of comfort, or self-importance, or whatever is making practice less genuine.

A beautifully written novel by Mark Salzman, *Lying Awake*, tells the story of a Carmelite nun who, after many years of dryness in her spiritual quest for God, begins to have intense mystical visions. But along with the visions, she begins having severe and increasingly frequent headaches. After consulting a doctor, she is diagnosed with epilepsy, which is commonly believed to promote mind-altering visions. Here is her dilemma: if the epilepsy in fact causes her higher states, does this mean that her contact with God is not "real"? What of all the beautiful poetry that she has written in these states, which has inspired so many others? Are her insights less genuine because they might be triggered by a neurological disorder?

What should she do? If she treats the epilepsy, she may lose her ability to experience closeness with God and return to her intolerable dry period, giving up the joy that is now part of her life. But if she doesn't treat the epilepsy, she'll become an increasing burden on the other nuns, who will have to care for her.

Her dilemma highlights the very difficult issues of faith and doubt. We all have the belief, the faith, that practice will take us in a certain direction. Over our lifetime this faith in practice will be tested repeatedly. Any honest practice will include periods of doubt. Questions will arise: "What am I really doing with my life?" "Am I just trying to get a little personal happiness and avoid suffering, or am I genuinely aspiring to know God?"

To persevere in our practice *knowing* that we don't know the answers to these questions is how we deepen our quest. As we stay with the doubt, as we rest in the discomfort of groundlessness, we can gradually see more clearly what our life is really about.

As long as we try to hold on to our false sense of ground, which we perpetuate through maintaining the safety of our self-images, the familiarity of our opinions, and the comfort of our habitual behavior strategies, we stay stuck in the self-centered life of "me and mine." Being willing to experience doubt when it arises gives us the opportunity to question what we're really up to. But this questioning can't be merely analytical. For it to transform us, it must be an *experiential* process.

When the nun in *Lying Awake* was able to stay with and truly experience her doubt, she understood the necessity of leaving the comfort of practice as she had come to know it. She was able to step out of her own personal suffering enough to truly include others. In extending herself to others—not from a sense of guilt or obligation, but from a taste of what her life was truly about—she began to find the answer to her crisis.

The dry spot isn't something that happens just to other people. We've all experienced moments when we lose all motivation to practice or forget why we ever began. We've all gotten caught in the trap of replacing the real efforts of practice with reading about it, thinking about it, talking about it. We've had dry periods when we've lost contact with our aspiration to awaken, when we've had little idea of what our life is really about. What is it about? This is the question we need to ask, knowing that we don't know the answer, yet willing to stay with the emotional and physical distress of not knowing. In staying with the dryness, the self-doubt, the uncertainty, we can gradually reconnect with our aspiration. In answering the question "What *is* life about?"—*experientially*—we will find the only real solution to the dry spot.

6
Thirty-one Flavors
of Practice

HERE ARE THIRTY-ONE ANSWERS to the question "What is practice?" You can choose one as a slogan to practice with each day. As you go through your day, hold it in your mind and use it to deepen your experiential understanding of what your life is about.

- Practice is about experiencing the truth of who we really are.

- Practice is about being with our life as it is, not as we would like it to be.

- Practice is about clarifying our belief systems so that even if they remain, they no longer run us.

- Practice is about seeing through the illusion of a separate self.

- Practice is about learning to be kind, but we will never be kind until we truly experience our unkindness.

- Practice is about attending to and experiencing wherever we're stuck, whatever we're holding, whatever clouds our True Nature.

- Practice is about willingly residing in whatever life presents to us.

- Practice comes back again and again to the basic koan: "What *is* this?"—always pointing directly to the experiential truth of the moment.

- Practice is about turning away from constantly seeking comfort and trying to avoid pain.

- Practice is about learning to be no one, not giving solidity to any belief system—just Being.

- Practice is about becoming free of the slavery of our self-judgments and our shame.

- Practice is about seeing through the false promise of our ideals and fantasies.

- Practice is about becoming a lamp unto ourselves.

- Practice is about moving from a life of emotional upset toward a life of equanimity.

- Practice is always about returning to our True Nature.

- Practice is about the growing ability to say thank you to everything that we meet.

- Practice is about the transformation of our unnecessary suffering.

- Practice is about the clash between what we want and what is.

- Practice is about increasingly entering into Love—not personal love, but the Love that is the nature of our Being.

- Practice is about turning from a self-centered view to a life-centered view.

- Practice is about finally understanding the basic paradox that although everything is a mess, All Is Well.

- Practice is about appreciating our preferences without making them demands.

- Practice is not about suffering, but *learning* from our suffering.

- Practice is about perseverance—the ability to continue in our efforts even though life doesn't please us in the ordinary sense.

- Practice is about learning to live from the open Heart—the Heart that only knows connectedness.

- Practice is about becoming free of our attachments and the suffering that is born of those attachments.

- Practice will always entail forgiveness, at least as long as there is even one person whom we can't forgive.

- Practice must ultimately deal with the most basic human fear, the fear of extinction, whether of the physical body or of the ego.

- Practice is about learning to say yes to what's happening, even when we hate it.

- Practice is about giving ourselves to others, but like a white bird in the snow.

- Practice always comes back to the *willingness to just be.*

PART TWO

Attachments and Ideals

7
Attachment

THE SUBSTITUTE LIFE is a very narrow way of living. This narrowness is rooted in our need to feel comfortable, to cling to what is familiar and safe. To avoid experiencing the anxious quiver at the core of our being, where we might feel the chaos of uncertainty or the pain of unhealed wounds, we weave a protective cocoon of beliefs and identities. Unfortunately, living in this way also cuts us off from the vastness of our True Nature, our naturally open heart.

The most troublesome beliefs are related to our attachments, which are often hard to identify. Attachments are simple beliefs—fantasies, in fact—that have become solidified as "truth" in our mind. They also partake of the energy of desire, which is based on the underlying belief that without some particular person or thing, we can never be free from suffering. Attachment also takes the form of avoidance; we believe we can't be happy as long as a particular person, condition, or object is in our lives. To experience negative attachment, just think of your least favorite food or person.

We all develop attachments to the persons or things we believe are essential to our happiness. Often we're more attached to our belief than we are to the actual person or thing. The belief fuels our anxious efforts to attain or keep this someone or something. If we succeed, we might experience an ephemeral excitement. But because we'll always be anxious about losing what we gained, our satisfaction is short-lived.

In order to practice with attachment, we have to first *see* our belief with clarity, precision, and honesty. Next, we have to see that not only is this belief false, but that clinging to it is the source of our unhappiness. It's *because* we are attached that we are unhappy.

For example, it's easy to see how we are attached to other people, truly believing that our happiness somehow depends on them. We can also easily see how we are attached to food, pleasure, or comfort. We maintain the belief that our emotional well-being is inextricably linked to having what we believe will make us happy. But holding these beliefs guarantees that we cannot be deeply satisfied, because we will always be anxious at the thought of losing what we believe makes us happy. If we wish to be really happy, we have to give up our attachments.

In other words, we have to make the choice between happiness and attachment. Do we want to be attached or do we want to be happy? The answer is very clear—we want to be attached! For example, even though we can see that our desires give us ephemeral pleasure at best, we still cling to them. We won't give up the *belief* that they will in fact eventually make us happy.

Will money or position make us happy in the sense of a deep or abiding satisfaction? Even when we experience that they won't, we often still pursue them, because we still *believe* that they could. Will another person make us happy? This is a little more difficult to see, because we all cling to the desire to feel appreciated, loved, secure, connected, and we *believe* that someone can provide this. Even when we see that someone can't give us what we want and require, we still *believe* they can! This belief *is* our attachment, the source of our suffering. As long as we see another person through the filter of our fear-based requirement that they make us feel a certain way, we are setting ourselves up for reaction and disappointment.

Do our core beliefs that we are unworthy, unlovable, and incomplete make us happy? Just the opposite, yet our attachment to our core beliefs remains one of the strongest attachments, and also one of the most difficult to see, because what we are attached to is so close to home. It's our defining identity as a self. We feel a sense of stability in the familiar, even when it makes us miserable.

We can find attachments everywhere: to our accomplishments, to identities based on how others see us, to our occupation, to where we live, to what kind of car we drive. We can certainly find our attachments to another person being a particular way, based on the belief that we need them to be a certain way for us to be happy. But love, or the happiness that we naturally derive from love, is not based on need. And to the extent that we are attached to the fulfillment of our needs, we cannot really love.

Freedom from attachment requires that we first *see* the ways in which we're attached. In particular, we have to see how attachments arise out of beliefs. For example, physical pain presents an opportunity to look at our attachment to comfort and the beliefs we hold around it. The belief that life should be free from pain might express itself in thoughts such as "This is too much" or "Nobody should have to put up with this." Underlying those thoughts is the belief that we can't feel happiness while we're feeling discomfort. I certainly used to believe this, but now I know that it simply isn't true. In fact, attachment to the belief that we can't be happy while in pain may be a greater source of suffering than physical discomfort itself. Until we see this belief for what it is, a belief that may not even be true, we'll remain attached to physical comfort, guaranteeing our dissatisfaction.

Sometimes it's difficult to see the strength of our attachments. During a recent talk on attachment, I told the audience that one or two people would be asked to come up front and sing their hearts out as they might do in the privacy of the car or shower. As soon as I said this, you could feel the tension rise. Many people later admitted that the thought of singing in public made them cringe. They weren't reacting to the singing;

singing usually feels good. They were reacting to the assault on their cherished self-image, which on some level we all believe is necessary for keeping us safe, secure, and together. *This* is our attachment. We'd often rather cling to it and suffer than give it up and be free.

To practice with attachment, we need to identify the beliefs inherent in our attachments; then we have to see how strongly we're holding on to them. We also need to understand that these beliefs are not the truth. It's also sometimes necessary to know why we're afraid to give them up. The example of singing in front of the group demonstrates our belief that maintaining a particular self-image is necessary to give us ground, to prop us up, and to hold the anxious quiver of being at bay. Holding on to our self-image protects us from taking the leap into the terror of the unknown.

Another example: Suppose I have the belief that without order and control, my life will be chaotic and unsafe. I become attached to this illusion of control, believing that it gives me security. But what am I really doing? I'm using the strategy of control to avoid experiencing the one core fear that terrifies me—the fear of helplessness resulting from loss of control. My attachment to control shields me from experiencing that primary fear. But in avoiding the fear, I forfeit the possibility of ever being free. Working with attachment requires that we start to drop our beliefs and enter into the experiential world. There we must face the terror of not having our belief-based identity to hold us up.

Much of my insight into the power of attachment came out of struggling with the intense identification I've had with my daughters. The most prolonged and fruitful struggle centered on the basketball career of my younger daughter, Jenessa. We had played basketball together since she was ten years old. By the time she reached high school, she was the star of her team. When she played well, I would feel great; but when she had the occasional off game, I would feel horrible. I tried to practice with these ups and downs, but she usually played well, so I was less motivated to explore my attachment since it usually felt good.

When Jenessa went to college, she had a great first year. But in the very first game of her sophomore year, she tore a knee ligament. She was sidelined for the remainder of the season. Although we were both disappointed, we could still look forward to the following year. But that season turned out to be very difficult. As hard as she worked, the year off had taken its toll; her body wasn't quite in sync with the game. The physical difficulties led to limiting beliefs that became mental difficulties. As I watched Jenessa struggle, I experienced in my gut the power of attachment.

Of course, as a father I naturally felt bad for my daughter. But that wasn't the problem. The problem was my attachment to her success. I was unknowingly living from the belief, the illusion, that my happiness depended on how well she played. My attachment to this belief was so strong that during and after the "bad" games, I would feel sensations of dread and doom in my stomach.

From the perspective of practice, it was good news that the disappointment was so strong: it really got my attention. I felt the extent and power of my attachment and how it imprisoned me. I started viewing Jenessa's games as an opportunity to study and work with attachment. When her game was off and I felt the sinking feeling and mild nausea of anxiety, I'd observe what beliefs gave rise to my emotional and physical reactions. Soon I began to see what was going on: I was attached to *my* accomplishments. Because I was so identified with Jenessa, seeing her as an extension of myself, I experienced her accomplishments and her "failures" as my own.

More specifically, I believed that my well-being depended on how successful or productive I (she) was. Without the prop of success, who would I be? I'd be left facing the core fear of failure—that hole of dread, shame, and hopelessness. Once my attachment became clear, I realized that only by entering this hole, by willingly residing in it, could I ever become free of its power. And so I would sit in the stands, trying to feel the texture and quality of the dread that before I'd just wanted to avoid.

Some beliefs and attachments are so closely held that clarity about them is very elusive. This is especially the case with our children. Our identification with them can be so strong that it takes time to clarify, *experientially*, that we are seeing them as extensions of ourselves. We need to be willing to experience the anxious quiver of being, no longer buffered from reality by the illusory belief in our attachments. When I began to open to the anxious quiver, which I had tried to cover over with Jenessa's successes, I realized how narrow and self-centered my interest in her had been.

As my attachment became clearer and its power diminished, I found that I could enjoy my daughter's efforts even when she didn't excel. During the last two years she played, I was grateful for being increasingly able to appreciate *her*, apart from my own neediness and attachment. Attachment is always a barrier to real appreciation and happiness, because it's based on the illusion that some external element can make our core pain go away. But when we're willing to expose ourselves to the pain we've been avoiding, the power of attachment fades and the path to a genuine life becomes more accessible.

I'm not talking about becoming totally free of attachment, but about loosening our clinging. We can move from the *demand* that we get some particular thing to the less emotion-based *preference* for that thing. For example, suppose we are attached to our health. If we become sick or disabled, especially for a long time, we may experience our attachment, at least in part, in the form of anger. Our attachment to a picture of how life should be, healthy in this case, takes the form of an emotion-based demand. When life doesn't meet this demand, we feel angry. Only as we work with our attachment can we see through the demands that we're placing on life. As the demand loses its hold, we can enjoy it as a preference. Having preferences isn't a problem, nor is enjoying them.

What is problematic, and what gives rise to suffering, is enslavement to our attachments to such an extent that they run our life.

The practice of working with attachment first requires that we experience the prison of our attachments.

Second, we have to see that we don't want to get out of this prison, that we prefer believing our beliefs to being free. Third, we have to observe ourselves and—with clarity, precision, and honesty—come to know all the beliefs that maintain a particular attachment.

Fourth, we need to see with equal clarity that our beliefs are not the truth; they are just beliefs. This is much easier said than done. It's at this point that we can understand why we hold on to our beliefs and why we're afraid to give them up. We begin to see how we use our beliefs as a shield against feeling our fears.

Then we must enter the experiential world, where we begin to drop our beliefs and allow the fear of losing our belief-based identity to arise. But who wants to reside in this sinking quiver of groundlessness? No one does. However, only when we're able to reside in the physical experience of groundlessness—no longer clinging to our believed thoughts—can we disconnect the circuitry of our conditioning and diminish the power of our attachments. But it may take a large dose of disappointment to make this understanding real.

In this way, we gradually begin to experience a genuine life, without the beliefs and beyond the terror. This is the path of practice. When we fully see through and experience our attachments, the result is freedom. When we see through our fears, the result is love. When we see without our filters, judgments, and desires, the result is appreciation and the quiet joy of being.

At any given moment, you can ask the questions: Where do my attachments lie right now? What someone or something do I believe I can't be content without?

8
Addictions and Precision in Practice

WHEN WE'RE STANDING in the muddy water of everyday life, practice is often not simple and clear. But part of our challenge is to bring a certain precision and impeccability to our efforts. That's why it's important to keep returning to the two basic aspects of practice: first, seeing through the mental process, with all its noise; and second, entering the nonconceptual silence of reality-as-it-is. As practitioners, we learn to honestly and relentlessly observe the mental or conceptual process— thoughts, emotional reactions, strategies, and fears—and then bring ourselves back again and again to the physical reality of the present moment.

Being precise means focusing on what gets in the way of clarity in practice. We need to focus particularly on the addictions that keep us encased in a substitute life: not the obvious addictions, like drugs or alcohol, but the more subtle addictions to which we all fall prey.

Let's start with our *addiction to comfort*. I'm talking about the ways we manipulate our experience in an effort to find comfort and avoid pain. We've all got it to some degree. What does yours look like? Does it manifest as avoiding sitting meditation when you don't feel like it, or as moving around during sitting even when the instruction is to sit still? Can you see it in your attachment to food or sleep or fantasizing?

What is the practice here? First, we have to see the ways in which we constantly seek comfort. Then we look at our mental process, beginning with noticing our most basic beliefs. For example, if we're sitting in meditation and feel agitated, we ask, "What is my most believed thought right now?" The answer might be, "Life should be comfortable" or "Life should be free from pain." Or, "I can't be happy if I'm in discomfort." We certainly believe that these thoughts are true; yet, many people have experienced that our happiness does not depend on being free of discomfort. In fact, it's our *belief* that we have to avoid discomfort that is one of our deepest sources of unhappiness. But to see through the beliefs that underpin our habitual attitudes and behaviors, we first have to know what they are. We need to label our thoughts with precision and clarity to see through the addictive quality.

Once we see these beliefs clearly, what is the *experiential* component? It's staying with the restlessness, the anxious quiver, the hole of discomfort out of which our addictions spring. Residing in the present moment when it's uncomfortable isn't necessarily easy, since we have a natural aversion to discomfort. This is one reason why having a daily meditation practice is helpful; through it we learn to stay with the experience of the body even when this experience doesn't please us. However, to really reside in physical discomfort, it's helpful to first identify our believed thoughts.

As we observe the mental process with precision, we come to see that we rarely take a breath without a thought or opinion or judgment going through our head. We begin to notice the extent to which we're *addicted to our thoughts.* Much of the mental activity is innocuous, just energy arising as mental concepts. But for most of us there's also a particular addictive pattern. Once we know clearly what it is, we can use simple generic labels, such as "planning," "conversing," "remembering," or "worrying," and then return to our immediate physical experience. Sometimes we have to label more precisely. For example, to get to the addictive quality of fantasizing, we could say, "Having a believed thought that I *must* fantasize." Identifying the addictive quality makes it easier to return to the physical sensation of craving.

Some addictive patterns are more pernicious than others. For example, the *addiction to self-judgments* is particularly hard to see. We all fall into the trap of taking such thoughts as truth. "After all these years I'm still doing that. I'll never get this. I'm hopeless. I'm a bad person"—judgments like these arise from our most deep-seated core beliefs; these are the fixed decisions we made about ourselves early in life when faced with the inevitable sense of separation and protectedness we all feel. These beliefs always have a negative cast, like a darkened lens through which we interpret "reality." These negative filters, the results of past unpleasant experiences, actually shape our reality, although they don't reflect reality directly or accurately. Beliefs such as "I'll never measure up," "I'll always be alone," "If people could really see me, they would see that I was nothing" may sound trivial, but their devastating power comes from the fact that their "truth" isn't open to question. We accept them as reality. Thus our life remains a dissatisfying puzzle.

It's important to label these thoughts precisely; otherwise we'll continue to believe them. When the judgments stay intact, what happens? They continue to run our life. Once we've seen the self-judgments for what they are—just opinions—we return to our experience and ask ourselves how it feels, physically, to hold on to them. Again, we need precision to stay with the sensations and to resist the temptation to think about them. If we get hooked back into our judgmental thoughts, we're likely to wallow in guilt and shame, eventually confirming the "truth" of the thoughts rather than experiencing the feelings.

This brings us to one of our strongest addictions: the *addiction to our emotional states*. Think about the last strong feeling you experienced. At the time, didn't it seem like reality? When we're caught in disheartenment, we really believe that we'll never be adequate, that we'll never fit in, that nothing will ever work out, and so on. When we're caught in anxiety or confusion, it's hard to realize that it is just a passing emotional state. These emotions feel solid and permanent. Because there's no particular comfort in them, they may not even feel like an addiction. They may feel more like a barrier between ourselves and our happiness. But they're only a barrier until we pass through them. Then we see that the emotional state is just a prop that holds together our identity, a support to which we're addicted.

Among the most difficult to discern is the *addiction to our identities*—who we think we are. At any given moment, we all have a mental concept, typically several, of who we are. Some identities are concrete, such as the identity of being a parent or a student. Some are more image-based; we see ourselves as being smart or nice or spiritual. Usually we're blind to our identities and, consequently, to their addictive quality. For example, if we have the identity of being a spiritual seeker, we may unknowingly get comfort from the identity of being part of something bigger than ourselves. Or we could have the comforting identity of being studious, hardworking, or deep. We certainly get a very juicy comfort in "being right" or in being busy and productive. Ask yourself, what is your identity right now? Can you feel its addictive quality? Can you sense how you cling to it for comfort?

The *conceptual* aspect of practice is seeing these difficult-to-see identities with clarity. The *experiential* aspect comes into play when our identities are threatened, when our strategies to hold ourselves together fail. Here we have the opportunity to work with the sense of groundlessness, where our props are no longer supporting us. Unfortunately, it's just the place we don't want to be, because it takes us back to the core pain of feeling unworthy, faceless, isolated. Yet, to willingly reside here allows us to discover that our core pain lacks solidity. Ultimately we see that what we've spent our whole life trying to avoid is simply a complex of believed thoughts, unpleasant sensations, and ancient memories. But we can't reach this understanding while we're clinging to the props of our identities. The essence of practice, really, is dropping the addiction to identities, learning to be no one.

I don't mean to set up a new ideal of "being no one special." We already have enough idealized pictures of who we're supposed to be. For example, how many of us have the view that the spiritual ideal is being able to face death or adversity without fear? Such a view still involves ideals and artificial identities. Real freedom is to face adversity without *having* to be free from fear; without the addiction to the identity of "fearlessness."

Of course, we're more *addicted to fear* than to fearlessness. Notice how much of the day you hold tightly to your fears, especially the fear of losing control. All of our "what if" thinking falls into this category: What if I don't do it right? What if it's painful? What if I look bad? Such thoughts are based more on wanting to control some imagined future than on what's happening now. It's crucial to identify these thoughts by asking the question, "What is my most believed thought right now?"

After seeing the thoughts, we just sit, experiencing what's happening right *now,* aware of the intense physical sensations of anxiety—the tightness, the queasiness, the narrowing down. We might ask the practice question or koan, "What *is* this moment?" What happens when we do this? Finding the answer is what practice is really about.

Again, the simplicity and clarity of practice amounts to this: first, we must see through the mental process, dropping the story line of "me." What is the story line of "me"? It's the addiction to our comfort and thoughts, to our self-judgments and emotions, to our identities and fears.

How can we drop the story line of "me"? In a recent baseball movie, a star pitcher is facing a star batter at a crucial point in the game. The pitcher is having a hard time focusing. He's thinking about what would happen if the batter got a hit. He's distracted by the fifty thousand fans shouting and waving.

Then he says to himself, "Clear the mechanism." All of a sudden the sound level in the movie drops into silence. Even though the fans are still moving and waving, you no longer hear them; this reflects what the pitcher is experiencing as he disengages from his own emotional noise. Then he says to himself, "Now just throw the ball to the catcher, like you've done a million times before." In "clearing the mechanism," he was turning away from his preoccupation with the mental noise of "me," from his fear-based thoughts about imagined results, about himself as a star, as someone special. Then he could enter the direct experience of simply throwing the ball.

Once we learn to stop focusing on our inner noise, we can "clear the mechanism" and drop the story line of "me." Then it becomes possible to enter the experiential, nonconceptual world, the silence of reality-as-it-is. This doesn't mean we won't have messiness in our life; it just means we won't be so addicted to it. We'll always be conditioned beings living in a conditioned world; but it's possible to learn to relate to the clouds of conditioning as just clouds, to see them more and more within the context of the sky. To do this we need the precision of practice. We need to see our addictions for what they are—believed identities, thoughts, and other mental constructs—and work with them. We also need to see them for what they aren't: the truth about who we are or what life is.

9
"Ah So"

THERE'S A FAMOUS STORY about the Zen master Hakuin, who was falsely accused of fathering the child of a local peasant woman. When presented with this accusation, and the child, he simply said, "Ah so," and took the child under his care. Some time later, after feeling guilt and remorse, the mother came to Hakuin and confessed the truth, begging for her child back. Hakuin again replied, "Ah so," and returned the child he had helped raise to its mother. This is the kind of story we all love to hear, partly because it reinforces our romantic notions of practice. It brings to mind the idealized images of how we'll behave when we've really "penetrated the practice."

We don't know if this event happened or not. It doesn't matter. What matters is whether we use this story to foster or to dispel our illusions about practice, particularly those that create a picture of what we're supposed to be like sometime off in the future when we "get it all together." The danger, of course, is that we'll always be trying to measure up to some picture of how we're supposed to be. But what's wrong with this? Don't we need to be inspired by others? Shouldn't we aspire to be like Hakuin? Won't this motivate us to make sincere efforts to change, to be detached and strong like this good monk?

The truth is, this story touches two different aspects of ourselves. It touches our aspiration, showing us that there *is* a bigger picture of life; but it also tickles our little mind, which immediately takes over with a new formula for getting away from the life we don't like very much. And certainly most of us do try to change, to fix ourselves, in this way. We follow our ego and our will, trying to fulfill one picture after another of what we see as the "spiritual life." Yet, in trying to change in this way, in trying to fulfill our numerous ideals, we are almost always turning away from the life that's right in front of us. Trying to measure up to ideals is just another subtle way of resisting our life as it is. It keeps us from *just being* with the life that we don't want—the one in which we're not detached and strong and full of compassion.

Hakuin could have refused the baby and offered instead to help the mother learn to care for it responsibly. But would we still like the story if there were no romantic ideal to latch onto? If the story depicted the mess of everyday life that moves so fast we can never pin it down with a formula like "Ah so," would it still appeal to us? It's only by staying in the muddy water of everyday life that we can learn real appreciation and practice. What's required is giving up the filters of our opinions and judgments, our ideals and expectations. But giving up our filters is what we least want to do, particularly when it comes down to our ideals about spiritual practice.

What ideals are you holding on to right now? What pictures and expectations do you bring to your practice? Do you still have the deep-seated belief that if you meditate long and hard enough, you'll find the key to the kingdom and be free of suffering? Do you at least expect to get re-centered or recharged when you meditate? Do you expect to become peaceful, or at least less confused? Do you have the picture that talking to a teacher will somehow alleviate your problems? Do you have the picture that your teacher should or shouldn't be some particular way? Again, what specific ideals are you holding on to right now?

The easiest way to spot these ideals is to look closely at emotional upsets related to your practice. Emotional distress is a signal that we're experiencing life through the filter of an ideal, a picture, or an expectation. In such a situation, we need only ask the question, "How is it supposed to be?" This question will point us to what pictures and requirements we're living from. The practice is to keep seeing how the pictures prevent us from being with what *is*. Then we return to our experience with the question, "How is it *really*?" This allows us to feel the quiver of anxiety that arises when we dare to be without the comfort of formulas and ideals. Thus we experience the groundlessness of not knowing where to turn or what is right. If we can stay in that open place, we'll discover the truth of the moment.

Who wants to do that? To be honest, none of us. We would prefer to live in the seeming comfort of our fantasies. But the path requires that we examine *all* of our pictures, including those we have about practice. So we ask ourselves, What is sitting in meditation really about? What is it that we're trying to do in spiritual practice? What about the forms and rituals of our particular practice tradition? There is no doubt they can help raise our aspiration; but, *in themselves*, these forms and practices have little to do with seeing the truth. They are not inherently magical, yet we often maintain magical thinking around them. What our sitting posture is, how or whether we bow, whether or not we wear robes, how we perform ceremonies—do we use these as a way to connect with what is, or as a way to hide? Do we feel comfort and security in maintaining the identity of "Zen student" or "Tibetan Buddhist," or in holding on to some romantic belief about spiritual practice? Do we find security in feeling part of something bigger, or in believing that we're doing the practice right?

Many of us who see ourselves as spiritual aspirants take on new or exotic names. Then, after striving for many years to become free, some of us also add a title to our name, a mark of our status and achievement. Do we use these well-intended names and titles to buy into still another identity—one that is more subtle and sophisticated, but an identity nonetheless? It's so easy to buy our own act that we can actually feel and believe that we're different because we're now a "Buddhist" or a

"Sensei." If we believe in these identities, they reinforce the very delusion we seek to dispel.

Do we use these forms and practices to avoid the anxious quiver of being? To avoid having no solid place to stand? To avoid the experience of not knowing how to be or what to do? The longer we are in a particular tradition, the easier it is to hide in the routines, in doing it right, and, especially, in the jargon. This is the way we try to maintain control, the way we avoid the present moment, the way we avoid our core pain.

But the real question is whether we use the various forms and practices to foster true understanding of what our life is about or to obscure it. The extent to which we *believe* in these forms, to which we identify with them, to which we find comfort and security in them, and especially to which we feel the need to defend them as the right or only way—to this extent they no longer foster an open or transformative practice.

So again, what ideals, what pictures, what expectations do you hold about practice? To what extent do they often remain below the level of awareness while still running the show? It is because we regard them as "spiritual" that they are so elusive. Yet, if we pay attention to our emotional reactivity—asking the question, "How is it supposed to be?"—we will be pointed in the direction of openness and clarity.

We *all* live out of pictures. Until we know what they are, we will continue to experience reality through the filter of these self-imposed mental constructs; we will continue to cut ourselves off from the clarity of knowing what our life is really about. This is our life job: to see and to learn. Notice your ideals and expectations. Watch your habitual patterns. Experience your emotional reactions. See them for what they are. This is the path to transformation and freedom.

10
Practicing with Money

A STUDENT ASKED a Zen teacher if he could study with him. The teacher told him that it would cost him five hundred dollars a month. Agreeing to pay, the student studied very hard for the next three months. But throughout this whole period he felt more and more angry until one day, in a state of total upset, he said to the teacher: "I shouldn't have to pay for spiritual practice. Why are you charging me so much money? It's just not right, and I can't study with you under these conditions."

He left the teacher and tried to study on his own. After a while he realized he still needed some guidance; so he found another teacher. In their first meeting, the student told the teacher how he had become resentful about having to pay the first teacher for practice, even though he had practiced hard. The second teacher replied, "Fine. You can practice with me, and we'll see how it goes. You don't have to pay me. In fact, even payment for retreats is optional."

Feeling relieved, the student began studying with his new teacher. But he soon noticed that he wasn't making as much effort as he had before. After several months, the teacher called him in and said, "I think it would be best if you didn't study with me anymore." A little stunned, the student asked, "Why, what's the matter?" The teacher responded, "You say you don't think you should pay for practice, yet your behavior shows that you're not willing to practice seriously unless you pay money for it."

How can this story help us understand our own situation? Does it point to our pictures of the relationship of money to practice? On the one hand, it may often seem that money and practice don't mix; on the other hand, we often place value on something in proportion to how much we pay for it.

Money issues, along with sexual issues, obviously play a dominant role in everyday life. Yet we rarely consider either of these issues in terms of practice. Money issues tend to be seen as not even worthy of "spiritual" consideration. But given how much of our daily life distress is related to finances, it is unfortunate that we tend to overlook this crucial area of practice. Money issues make an especially rich field for practice, because our relationship to money is predominantly determined by unconscious beliefs and behaviors. Money issues rarely are just about money.

We have to come back again and again to the point of practice. The point of practice is freedom—freedom from the constraint of *all* our views, our identities, our constructs, our strategies. What good is it to sit in meditation, even if we're having great experiences, if we plunge into the anxiety of our financial situation as soon as formal practice ends? Practice includes everything, even the mundane world of money. Until we are free from our deep-seated beliefs about money, as well as our deeply conditioned behaviors, we cannot truly be free.

What's the practice here? It begins with knowing what we're up to, by precisely observing our believed thoughts around money. We can begin to discover them by asking ourselves questions such as the following: Do I experience tightness and anxiety around money issues? Do money issues provoke feelings of losing control, chaos, danger, or doom? If so, what strategy do I fall into: excessive frugality, frantic obsessing, withdrawal into hopelessness? How much of this strategy is based on fear-based projections that have almost no relationship to what's actually happening right now?

In terms of financial issues, think of your own examples: not getting the job you want, losing the job you have, having difficulty paying a mortgage, not being able to pay bills, losing money on the stock market, being threatened by a lawsuit, or enduring the financial chaos of divorce. Being in any one of these situations is likely to bring up many emotion-based believed thoughts. We also have our characteristic ways of coping, conditioned strategies to deal with financial difficulties. Our practice has to begin with realizing that identifying and working with these very beliefs and strategies *is our practice.* Then we can begin to observe and practice with anxiety instead of just blindly reacting to it.

Even when anxiety isn't right on the surface, it may still be running the show. For example, do you see money as simply a source of diversion, to be spent freely as an entertainment? You could even do this under the guise of being free, perhaps expressing and believing the thoughts, "I'm spontaneous, because I'm not constricted with worries about money." If you feel this way, once you really look at what you're doing, you may begin to see how your spending is in fact an effort to escape the present moment, to numb the anxious quiver of being.

Some of us have the view that money is somehow impure; this is the legacy of the American Puritans, who separated money from the "spiritual," creating a false dichotomy of money versus morals. Perhaps you hold a watered-down version of this in the belief "Have not, want not." This advice to live simply may sound Zen-like, but as long as it's a conditioned belief rooted in fear, we're still living from the requirement that life *should* be a certain way. In that case, we are certainly not free. We must use the dispassionate, yet engaged eye of practice to ferret out beliefs we blindly hold.

We're all products of our cultural roots. In the United States, many of us are still living out of conflicting beliefs from Puritan and Calvinist cultural values. A little-known fact is that the Puritans wanted a more open society in which people took care of each other. The emphasis was on spiritual rather than material wealth. Right alongside this Puritan strain ran the Calvinistic, or Protestant, work ethic, which emphasized individual effort and materialism. As products of our culture, we can't possibly avoid the contradictory values of these two strong influences.

Here's a joke that illustrates this point. A new member of a church congregation approaches the preacher after the sermon and says, "That was a damned good sermon today, Preacher!" The preacher solemnly replies, "We don't use words like that around here. We don't curse in this congregation." The new person responds, "I don't know what to say—it was just such a *damned* good sermon." The preacher indignantly replies, "I'm sorry, but if you want to be a member here, you can't talk like that." The member shrugs and says, "Okay, but it was such a damned good sermon that I wrote you a check for five thousand dollars and put it in the kitty." And the preacher exclaims, "No shit!"

The more we observe ourselves, the more it becomes clear that there are many "me's," which often contradict each other. Some of us hold the perhaps unconscious view that money is somehow impure, and at the same time value things only in proportion to what we pay for them. What's important is to be precise in our self-observation, clearly labeling our beliefs about money. Some examples: "Once I get my money situation under control, I'll be safe and able to relax." "I'll never be able to take care of myself." "It's better to spend in a carefree manner and have fun than to be uptight and frugal." "It's better to be frugal than to be careless about spending and about the future." Each of these examples not only indicates a different belief in relation to money, but also points to a particular set of strategies about how to cope with life. And with each belief and strategy that we blindly adhere to, we restrict and narrow our life.

It's only through endlessly *observing* our beliefs and behaviors that such patterns can be uncovered. And then what? Do we try to change them? Suppose, for example, we see that we are stingy, acting out of the fear of scarcity. Do we then try to be generous? That would certainly be our habitual tendency, but it has nothing to do with practice. We'd only be acting from relentless self-judgment, trying to change and fix ourselves. The only thing we have to change is our awareness. The practice is first to see clearly our beliefs and strategies. Then we need to locate the well of fear from which they arise. Finally, we must learn to gradually welcome the experience of fear into our awareness, especially the fear of losing control, of not feeling safe and in charge.

Inviting fear in is never easy, because we instinctively move away from its unpleasantness. Yet it is vital to open willingly to our blind tendencies and hidden swamps of fear. Opening in this way requires courage, but the effort is not a strong-armed one. We don't have to tighten in a struggle against ourselves. Instead, we need the softer effort of compassion, which comes from seeing our conditioning as *just* our conditioning.

Without this kind of effort, where are we? What are we really doing? We can't exclude any area of our life from practice, nor can we forget that we always have to pay the price for what we do. The price may not be monetary, but it still needs to be paid. So ask yourself, "What is the price of practice?"

11

Groundhog Day

IN THE MOVIE *Groundhog Day*, the main character wakes up every morning in the same exact place, at the same exact time, always having to repeat the same day—Groundhog Day. No matter what he experiences, he still wakes up having to repeat the day. No matter what he does, he can't get what he wants, which in this case is the sexual conquest of his female colleague. Although he tries all of the classic strategies of escape, nothing works; he still wakes up the next day to the same mess.

In the meantime, another part of him is growing. He starts moving from just trying to fulfill his own desires to doing things for other people. For example, every day he saves the same child from falling out of the same tree at the same time. He even starts using his once ego-driven accomplishments, such as playing the piano, to entertain others, not just to serve himself. Finally, not through purposeful effort or even awareness, he becomes more and more life-centered, less and less self-centered. And in typical Hollywood fashion, he gets the girl. However, his real success lies in breaking free from the repeating patterns of his personality.

One of the themes of practice is the gradual movement from a self-centered life to a more life-centered one. But what about our *efforts* to become more life-centered—doing good deeds, serving others, dedicating our efforts to good causes? There's nothing wrong with making these efforts, but they won't necessarily lead us to a less self-oriented life. Why? Because we can do these things without really dealing with our "self." Often our efforts, even for a good cause, are made in the service of our desires for comfort, security, and appreciation. Such efforts are still self-centered, because we're trying to make life conform to our pictures of how it ought to be. It's only by seeing through this self—the self that creates and sustains our repeating patterns—that we can move toward a more life-centered way of living.

Often our natural impulse to do good deeds is confused with other motives. This is not surprising, considering how often we're given the message, especially in our early years, that to *do* good means to *be* good. In being told we're good when we're helpful, we receive the praise we crave. Yet once we confuse helpful behavior with our own needs, we're locked into a pattern that undermines our genuine desire to do good.

When I was six years old, I lived in an apartment house on the boardwalk in Atlantic City, New Jersey. My father owned a retail store about two miles down the boardwalk. During the tourist season he would work fourteen hours a day. Since he couldn't come home for supper, every night my mother would make him a hot meal and put it in a brown paper bag. My job was to carry this bag in the basket of my tricycle and deliver it to my father while it was still hot. I can still see myself—a very earnest little boy single-mindedly speeding down the boardwalk on my tricycle so that my father could have a hot supper. There's no doubt that I felt a natural desire to do good. But somewhere along the line, perhaps from repeatedly being praised as a "good boy," my natural desire to do good became enmeshed with getting my father's approval and love.

We all have our own version of this syndrome, because when we're children, we have a biological imperative to maintain the approval and love of our caregivers, whatever it takes. The problem arises when, as adults, we're still living out of the same old pictures—particularly of how we *should* be—without awareness of what's behind our need to help. Do we need to be seen as a helper? Do we need to feel and believe that we are, in fact, a helper? Do we need to see people as benefiting from our "help"? Or do we serve in order to be seen as a worthy person? Are we helping out of a sense of "should"? Can we see how attached we are to our "self," our self-image, our identity? Who would we be without it? What hole are we trying to fill with it? How are we trying to avoid the insecurity of groundlessness?

When our cover identity starts breaking down because the hole isn't being filled—for example, when we don't get the recognition that we want or the results that we hope for—we react emotionally, with some form of disappointment or anxiety. This reaction is an infallible practice reminder that we're still attached in some way. We've gone from being a helper to experiencing the core hole of helplessness. But we must reside in and practice with this helplessness in order to become free.

Most of our life is spent using behavioral strategies to cover or avoid our pain—the deep sense of basic alienation that takes the form of feeling worthless, hopeless, or fundamentally flawed in some way. When our strategy is to help, when we *need* to be helpful, this requires that we need to find people who seem helpless, or situations that seem to call for help. It's true that we may also have a genuine desire to help—one that isn't based on *our* needs—but whenever we feel an urgency or longing to help, it's often rooted in the fear of facing our own unhealed pain. If our basic fear is that we'll always be alone, what better way to avoid it than to find someone who needs us? If we have an underlying feeling of worthlessness, how better to prove that we're worthy than by doing good deeds? If we're trying to avoid the feeling of being fundamentally powerless or ineffectual, doesn't it make sense to take on the identity of someone who can affect people and outcomes positively through service?

The "helper" syndrome I'm describing is not outwardly harmful. What makes it dangerous is its potential to keep us blind to what is really going on. Yet it's easy to see how this lack of awareness, multiplied throughout our society, could lead to the social and political chaos that we live in. Failure to work with our inner turmoil—our need for power, our self-centered desires to possess, our fear-based greed and need to control—results in hatred, aggression, and intolerance. This is the source of all conflicts and wars. Without *inner* understanding, individuals as well as societies will continue to flounder. This is why it is so important for each of us to come back again and again to the practice of awareness.

We first must recognize that we're using our identity to live a life based primarily on finding some measure of comfort and security. But we also have to experience the core pain out of which this drive arises. The more we can learn to reside in this core pain, the more we connect with our innate compassion. Interestingly, this experience may not manifest as what we conventionally consider compassion. There is one story of a seeker who, upon clearly seeing the truth—where he was no longer defined and confined by his self-images—became a cab driver. Like a white bird in the snow, he was able to give himself to others simply through his own presence, his *being*. There was nothing special about his situation.

The question is: Where in our life do we do good, at least in part to subtly solidify the self? Where do we get in our own way? Where do we use even our identity as a spiritual seeker, or the comfort of being part of something bigger, to cover the anxious quiver of being?

In a way, we all keep waking up to the same repeating day, living our hazy notion of life—often clouded by our unending confusion and anxiety. Simply doing good deeds, or even being a devoted meditator, doesn't mean anything without the painful honesty that's required to look at what we're doing. We must take our heads out of the ground and look at all of the ways we get in our own way—fooling ourselves and obstructing the possibility of living a more open and genuine life.

PART THREE

Relationships

12

Relationships

WHY DO HUMAN BEINGS find relationships so hard? Many of
the difficulties we experience in life come directly from our relationships—not just with our mates, but with our parents,
children, teachers, bosses, friends. In short, with virtually anyone from whom we want something. This is a key point; almost all of our relationship difficulties come from wanting
something or *someone* to be different. Considering the amount
of suffering that arises from relationships, it's surprising that
the Buddha didn't include them in his list of the primary
causes of suffering, along with sickness, old age, and death.
One thing is certain: relationships, like serious illnesses, push
us right to the edge of where we're stuck. Stephen Levine has
noted that relationship, though not the easiest method for
finding peace, is certainly the most effective for discovering
what blocks it.

The fact that relationships often bring the most painful and
unhealed aspects of our life out of the shadows makes them a
potentially powerful teacher. But let's be honest, who actually
wants such a teacher? What do we really want from relationships? We want what we want! We want someone to fulfill our
needs, someone who will make us feel good, give us security,
appreciation, affection, and love. We also want our relationships, at least in part, to mask our core pain: the anxious quiver
of being that cries out for relief. But the more we rely on our relationships to either gratify our needs or assuage our pain, the

more we solidify our suffering. Another person can never heal our core pain; we can only do that for ourselves. But that doesn't keep us from asking others to do it. And when we don't get what we want, the messiness of relationship begins.

As soon as a conflict arises and we feel threatened in some way, we tend to forget all about relationships as a vehicle of awakening. We tenaciously hold on to our views, judgments, and need to be right. We protect and defend our self-image. We close down or lash out. And, believing in all these reactions as the unquestioned truth, we perpetuate our suffering. As we continue to do this, the disappointment we cause ourselves and others becomes a pain we can't ignore. That's the beauty of relationships as spiritual practice. The pain motivates us to awaken; disappointment is often our best teacher. This is when practice can really begin. But this view of relationships is very different from what we have been taught.

We were taught that relationships are supposed to give us security or save us. We usually assume that they're supposed to make us feel good through being supported, appreciated, loved, nurtured, or pleasured. We imagine that being in a relationship will relieve us of our loneliness.

That's how we approach relationships. Based on these expectations, requirements, and desires, we want something. We need, or think we need, the other person to *be* a certain way, to make *us* feel a certain way—safe, happy, or whatever. "I care for you" often means "I need you." We care for others as long as they satisfy our particular need, as long as they make us feel some special way. That's the setup.

This setup may be okay for a while, but what happens when we don't get what we want? Often we feel pain, anger, and resentment. We feel fear. In many cases, we go directly into blame, self-justification, and power struggles, trying to change the other to suit us. What we're really trying to do is change the other person so that they meet our expectations, our pictures. What gets us into trouble is that we almost always evaluate the other person's behavior according to *perceived* promises we believe this person made to us. These promises are, of course, simply our projected expectations. We then imagine that these promises are being broken, when in fact they were never made.

Suppose our expectation is that someone should take care of us. When we realize that it's not happening, we interpret this as an intentional act against us and instinctively react as if we were in real danger. We erect barriers of protection, or we attack in order to defend ourselves. It doesn't matter that this power struggle arose from our own expectations. We all engage in relationship difficulties on this level, where we struggle to get what we think we need or were promised. It may take us a long time to see that it leads only to endless suffering.

We view these difficulties as impediments to our happiness, even as obstacles to our spiritual path. We usually approach them by asking one basic question: How can I fix this? But we're missing the point: these obstacles, these difficulties, *are* our path.

Take, for example, the people who are embarrassing to you. They're either too fat or too thin, too talkative or too shy, too uptight or too loose—too *something*. What do you do when you see or think about these people? Most of us judge them, react, and use our discomfort as a justification to try to change them. We don't see that the problem is *ours*; *we're* requiring that *they* be a particular way. More to the point, it's not just our problem, it's our path, our way to wake up to a more genuine life.

Difficulties such as these are examples of emotion-based demands. Whenever we have an emotion-based demand in a relationship, it's a signal that there's practice to be done. But we need to be willing to practice, even though it may be painful to face our unhealed grief and core fears, which are likely to arise when we realize that our expectations and requirements aren't being met. The practice is to move from emotion-based demands, with the suffering they entail, to preferences. This involves acknowledging that while we would *prefer* life, or a person, to be a certain way, our loving them doesn't depend on their meeting these conditions. In this way, we move toward unconditional love, by working with everything that we ourselves add that blocks love. Removing the conditions we impose is how we open ourselves to the real love that already connects us with everyone. Transforming our emotion-based demands into preferences allows love to move freely and to come forth naturally.

But we have to see what we add that obstructs the free flow of a more open relationship. Don't all of us have expectations of how a relationship should make us feel? Don't we all have requirements of how another person must be? Don't we get lost in our beliefs, wanting to be right, trying to change the other person to meet our expectations? Aren't we so identified with others that we use them to fulfill our needs? In these ways, we launch ourselves into the inexorable collision course known as the power struggle. To the extent that we're not aware and that we mechanically act out our conditioning, we're bound to follow this predictable path. When two people who don't know themselves reach the point of conflict, the result is like a collision of machines. This collision is almost always blinding, for even though it may be easy to see how unaware the *other* person is, our own blind spots are blind by definition. Yet these conflicts are clues that we're in the dark. Reacting or, more specifically, *believing* in our reaction, is a sign that we're at least partially blind to what's really going on.

Take, for example, a couple who come together in the blinding passion of romantic love. Each has needs and personal "requirements"—for attention, for care, for appreciation. In the beginning it may seem that they can fulfill each other's requirements. But disappointment inevitably arises as the bloom fades and it becomes clear that satisfying the other's needs is not the main priority of each partner.

This scenario boils down to basic mechanics. One person, blindly driven by their own perceived needs, meets another person who is equally driven by mechanical needs. When their needs aren't met, they clash. Don't most power struggles result when we imagine that the other is reneging on a promise to give us what we think we need—a promise that was never made? As we react in fear, hurt, and anger, we pit ourselves against the other, as if the other were our enemy. Bringing awareness into a relationship involves seeing our tendency to project expectations and seeing our blind reactions when these expectations aren't met. We can then use reactivity as a signal to awaken from our blind, mechanical behavior. This is how we begin to practice.

To do this, we first have to learn to stop blaming others when we find ourselves in the middle of an emotional upset or conflict. This involves realizing that *all* of our emotional distress comes from something we ourselves add to the situation. This might be easy to know intellectually, but it's very hard to remember and apply in the middle of a conflict. We need to learn to listen to ourselves, to recognize that statements like "I can't stand it when he does that," "Nobody should have to put up with this," "This isn't right," and "This isn't fair" are our own deeply believed thoughts, not objective truths. This is how we begin to experience the pain of our protective stance. This is how we use it as an opportunity to practice with our own distress, even though we want nothing more than to blame it on someone or something else.

When we understand that we need to face our own "stuff" and work with it, we begin to naturally incorporate certain questions into our practice. As we learn to feel the physical tension of our emotional reactions, to hear ourselves wanting to blame, to see how much we want to believe our reactive thoughts, we begin to ask ourselves, "What's actually going on right now?" "How are things 'supposed' to be?" These questions point us toward our *own* expectations, requirements, desires, and fantasies.

Often they'll lead us to our most deeply held beliefs, such as, "I'm hopelessly flawed" or "I'm unworthy of love." Beliefs like these are always based on ancient memories and unhealed pain. Once we stop blaming and defending, once we begin to see these deeply held beliefs with some clarity, we're left with the one thing we least want to experience—the quivering core of pain that we've spent our life trying to avoid. We've used even our best relationships, at least in part, to mask this pain. Now we come face to face with what is. We experience the groundlessness and fear of exposing our pain without our defensive strategies. This is how working with relationships can bring us to the very heart of the practice life.

How do we do this? We begin to listen, to see. We stop keeping score. Most of all, we stop expressing angry feelings whenever they arise and instead try to be aware, to *experience*. We start to notice how enslaved we are to our expectations, requirements, desires, and unhealed pain. We start to see how our anger is often born out of fear. We begin to see fear as a key issue underlying most of our relationship difficulties. Fear of what? Our most basic core fears might include fear of being alone, of being rejected, of the unknown, of not getting what we want, of losing what we have, of intimacy, of being overwhelmed, of losing control, of being controlled, of having our inadequacy and unworthiness exposed. We begin to see how our particular core fears underlie the protective strategies that we employ. Think of your own situation. What is the fear? Here is where we come to the heart of practice, learning to stay present with the core quiver of pain that lies directly under almost all of our relationship conflicts.

Say, for example, we are hurt by someone's words or actions. We feel misunderstood, betrayed. This taps directly into our core pain, our core fears, reinforced by layer after layer of painful memories, stored throughout our very cells. These cellular memories are activated instantaneously, and we are caught in a reaction far out of proportion to the actual event. It's at this point that we normally either repress our negative reaction and seethe internally, or express it by lashing out externally. In either case, we're fully defended, with all of our justifications and blame.

But as we pay more attention to what's actually going on, becoming aware of repeating thoughts based on our deep-seated beliefs, practice begins. Knowing our thoughts is important, but in itself it cannot touch our cellular memory of pain. Only by directly experiencing our core pain—not as a concept, but as a complex of bodily sensations—can we go to the heart of practice. It is here, beyond forced effort, beyond thinking, that we reside in the "whatness" of our being in that moment. This residing in the moment allows transformation to take place. As we become less defended and more open to what is, we see that what we so feared is just a collection of thoughts, memories, and sensations. Simply resting in being, beyond the narrow identification with "me," we can now begin to really enter into relationship. Once we begin to face our unhealed core pain, to truly *experience* it, we're no longer enslaved by hidden agendas. No longer must we continue the painful life of reaction, defense, and endless suffering.

When difficulties arise around relationships and we're pushed to the edge of where we're stuck, we often seek traditional remedies to avoid the groundlessness we feel. We might think, "If only I could find the right person, I wouldn't feel so utterly lonely." Loneliness, however, is yet another opportunity to enter the heart of practice. We do this by experiencing, by residing in, our deep need to be loved. This differs from wallowing, from self-indulging, in that we don't believe the thoughts. Rather than getting lost in the controlling mind's need to know why we're lonely or how to fix it, we ask, "What *is* this loneliness?" and stay with our bodily experience. We stay by sending a compassionate awareness into the place we least want to be, and residing there.

Sometimes loneliness may feel so uncomfortable that we think we can't stand it for another second. In those moments, we bring awareness to the "heartspace"—the center of the chest—breathe in and out of that area. With each inbreath, we breathe the loneliness directly into the heartspace; with each outbreath, we simply exhale, with no intent to do or get rid of anything. We keep taking just *one more breath* into the center of the chest. This is how we find the courage to go on, even if it's only for one more breath. As we stay with the loneliness, as we stop pushing it away and instead allow it in, the hole of loneliness gradually heals. Instead of forever seeking *someone* to cover this hole, we learn that it's even okay to invite the loneliness in. We learn that inviting it in is far less painful than trying to push it away or using a relationship to anesthetize it. It gradually becomes clear that willingness to let the loneliness just be is the only genuine path for transcending loneliness.

This whole process goes against everything we've been taught. No longer are we just seeking comfort and protection. No longer are we expecting relationships to save us. No longer are we seeing our conditioned difficulties as flaws to be fixed. No longer are we trying to approach our distress through thinking and analysis. We've never been taught what it means to really experience our lives. Mostly we just *think* about what we're experiencing. And, of course, we believe our thoughts are reality.

Perhaps all of this sounds bleak. Perhaps it seems like a one-sided view of relationships as dark and heavy. What about the joy of relationship? Perhaps we'd rather just lighten up and forget about dealing with our pain and fear. The answer to this is obvious: if we *could* simply lighten up and find joy in our relationships, we would. But to the extent that there is suffering in our relationships, or to the extent that even our good relationships could become better, to this extent we need to work honestly with our blind spots and stuck places.

In theory, practice can seem so straightforward, so simple. We notice what is actually going on, we try to be aware, we try to fully experience what is, then we stop trying and just be. But when we're standing in the muddy water of life, the clarity and simplicity of practice is often lost. This is certainly true of relationships, which in pushing us to our edge, put us in a place where it's often difficult to even consider practice. Being caught in emotion-laden thoughts—"What about *me*?", "What about *my needs*?", "I get *so* tired of this", "This isn't fair"—makes it particularly difficult to extricate ourselves from our beliefs. But as our aspiration to awaken becomes stronger, we can learn to practice even in moments when we're most trapped. It's in these moments that we can come to know real joy in relationship, not just the superficial security of seeking psychological safety.

The religious philosopher Søren Kierkegaard said that perfect love is to love the one through whom one has become unhappy. To put it another way, the more we work with our own reactions, the more the path is cleared for love to simply flow through us. The more we remove the conditions we impose on our relationships, the more open the way to unconditioned love. We don't have to open our hearts. The heart is already open. We just need to clear the obstructions that get in the way of experiencing that openness.

Working with our own reactions takes on a particularly interesting twist because what we want most from another is often what is most difficult for them to give. The converse is also true: what's most difficult for us to give is often what another wants most from us. This illustrates exactly what Kierkegaard meant by perfect love being the love that comes from our unhappiness. If we see that we're stuck in not wanting to give someone what they want, and if we're willing to work with the layers of anger and fear around our stuck condition, then it becomes the path to freedom. To counteract fear-based withholding might require intentional acts of generosity, not in order to be virtuous, but to push ourselves to the edge in order to face our fears. The more honestly and clearly we see and experience our fears, the less they will dictate our behavior.

As we give—and work with what gets in the way of giving—we heal. Over time, generosity becomes our natural inclination. Healing ourselves in this way indirectly also heals the other by giving them the option of slowly lowering their own protective barriers. This differs from trying to change the other, from getting them to give us what we want. Practice is about working on ourselves only, on our own unhappiness. Yet each effort to bring spaciousness around our own fears allows spaciousness to open around the other's fears as well.

When Elizabeth and I came together as a couple, I was struggling with my propensity to be critical and judgmental. I'd seen the harm that this tendency had done in the past, and I knew that I needed to work with it. It was also clear that Elizabeth was not the least bit interested in being fixed. I made it my practice to avoid criticizing her as much as possible. At first it was difficult, because what is an ego if not a collection of opinions, identities, and judgments—all of which we believe? When a judgment about another crosses our mental screen, we normally accept it as the truth, and it's hard to keep our mouth shut.

In making the effort to not express my critical judgments, I learned something amazing. My judgments were never about her, they were always about me! The perfect example of this lies in our different styles regarding possessions. I like owning very little. Elizabeth, on the other hand, enjoys finding thrift-store treasures. It's not that she's materialistic; it's just that her joy comes with bringing home a load from the Goodwill, whereas my joy comes from being able to throw something out. What I do own, I like to keep neat and orderly, while Elizabeth likes having all her stuff out there where she can see it.

It may seem that my style—being simple, neat, and orderly—is more Zen-like. Before I met Elizabeth, I certainly believed this to be true. But when I started practicing withholding my critical judgments, I began to see things quite differently. When I'd see Elizabeth's style, instead of telling her how much better it would be for her if she were more orderly, I began to pay attention to the emotional state from which my judgments were arising. Had I simply expressed my judgments, I would never even have seen my own inner state. And what did I see? I saw fear. I saw my own fear of chaos. My preference for orderliness and neatness was not so much a Zen virtue as a strategy of control—a way of avoiding my fears of chaos, helplessness, and losing control.

Seeing this clearly made it easy to avoid expressing my judgments to Elizabeth. I understood that what I needed to do was tend to my own discomfort. Ordinarily, we assume it's the other person's job to take our discomfort away. From a practice point of view, nothing could be further from the truth. Our discomfort is *our* job. For example, when we experience the fearful quality of jealousy, it's our job to tend to it, not someone else's job to take it away by changing their behavior. When we experience the fear of insecurity around money issues, it's our job to rest there, not another's job to make our fears go away. What's so interesting about human dynamics is that once we attend to our job—seeing our beliefs and experiencing the fears from which they arise—it usually frees the other to move toward us. When the other no longer feels the need to defend, they become more willing to attend to *their* job.

Try the following exercise: Pick someone you have a lot of judgments about, preferably someone with whom you have frequent contact. Then choose one day a week; and for the entire day, from the time you wake up until you go to bed, withhold all judgments and criticisms of the other person, even the ones you silently think (and believe are true). Whenever the judgments arise, notice them, but don't solidify them by thinking or speaking them. Instead, try to experience the physical tension that is the bodily component of the held belief.

This exercise isn't designed to change our behavior or to suppress our emotions. It's designed to allow us to *see*. In giving nonjudgment to another, which is what everyone wants and also one of the hardest things to give, we're actually giving ourselves a great gift. This gift is the opportunity to see that our judgments and criticisms are always more about us than about the other person. This understanding gives us a context in which we can work more easily and directly with our deepest fears and attachments. It may take several weeks of doing this exercise to see its real value.

On the path of awakening, one of the most basic assumptions is that we have an inner quest to awaken—that our True Nature strives to reveal itself. Though we sense this in ourselves, we often forget that the same thing is happening in others. We probably understand, at least in moments of clarity, that we ourselves are doing the best we can. But we often forget that this is also true of others. When we relate to others from our small mind, with its desires and judgments, we relate only to the small mind of the other. This is how we stay caught in our self-centered life—a life that guarantees suffering.

When we relate to another from the bigger mind, we relate to their deepest nature as well. We can see how they too, even while caught in their small mind's needs, are doing the best they can. Often this is hard to see. Especially in the midst of a difficult relationship, we can't even see it in ourselves. We have to continually remind ourselves that difficulties *are* the path and that we'll often be blind to them. They aren't flaws to be fixed, or obstacles to be surmounted, but simply the stuff of a conditioned life, from which freedom can gradually emerge. The more we understand our own difficulties as the path, the more we can understand that the difficulties of others are also their path. The more we practice with our own pain, the more we learn that pain is not our enemy. The more we learn not to judge it as a defect, the more understanding we can be in relating to the pain of others.

When Elizabeth and I were married, the one essential vow we made was to remember that each of us had the wish to awaken. The practice is to remember, even in the midst of difficulty, that the other's inmost desire is also to become free from illusion. To assume this wish in another allows us, especially in those moments when hurt and fear arise, to stop the protective tendency to blame or to fix the other; instead, we return to our job, which is to clarify and experience our own fears. To assume that another wishes to awaken is certainly difficult at times, but to whatever extent we can relate from our deeper nature, we make genuine relatedness possible.

As we continue to clarify our beliefs, expectations, and requirements, and as we bring awareness and loving-kindness to the layers of pain that we must ultimately face and experience, we can gradually find the joy in relationships that we all seek. This joy isn't the result of getting what we thought we needed. Joy in relationships comes from being in contact with our essential connectedness, which most naturally expresses itself through generosity. Nietzsche, addressing the sun, wrote, "Oh great star, what would your happiness be if you had not those for whom you shine?" This is a far cry from giving in order to get—or even from giving with the intent of giving. The joy in relationships ultimately comes from effortlessly giving ourselves to others, like a white bird in the snow.

13

Trust

TRUST IS ONE of the trickier issues we meet in practice. When trust issues arise, the feelings are usually quite intense; they carry a lot of juice. Thoughts like, "I can't trust him anymore," "I feel betrayed," and "I feel like I was stabbed in the heart with a knife" can seem very true, very valid, very justified. Yet, what we often miss with such thoughts is the degree to which we're blaming others for our own reaction.

When we feel betrayed by someone or something we once trusted, and withdraw in anger, what's actually going on? Our sense of "self" has been shaken. The rug has been pulled out from under our secure ground of expectations and projections. We experience the fear of groundlessness; we feel the loss of safety with the loss of our identity. We usually react with hurt and anger. Our core fears are aroused. Losing trust in someone sets off the fear of being abandoned or the fear of being overwhelmed.

We think we have the right to ask others to protect us from our core fears, but in fact, none of us has that right. We think we *must* be able to trust; but what we consider "trust" is simply an effort to secure a picture of the world that is based on our desire for comfort and safety. To live in the illusion of this security is to live a substitute life.

What does it mean to say, "I trusted him, but now I know I can never trust him again"? Which picture of "him" can't we trust anymore? Our desire to view the self as a solid entity is so great that we miss the readily observable fact that the "self" is no more than a collection of self-images, identities, beliefs, strategies, memories, and projections. As we observe ourselves over and over, we come to see how quickly this "me" can change even from one minute to the next. No matter how firm and resolute we are in making decisions and commitments, another "me" will often arise, one who wants nothing to do with them. To appreciate the fluidity of "me," we need only look at our New Year's resolutions, our endless diets, and other futile efforts to modify our behavior. We finally get the picture that the seemingly solid "I" is really many "me's" who frequently disagree. So why do we think that other people are any different? Isn't our picture of the "other" based mostly on a combination of our memories and wishful thinking, as well as on the projections that come out of that?

When we first meet someone, we think we see them as they are. But we're not seeing them as *they* are; we're seeing them as *we* are. We're seeing them through the filter of all our associations, expectations, and projections. Over time, as we begin to see them with fewer filters, we feel betrayed: "You're not the person you were when we first met!" Of course they're not—in fact, they never were! Yet we hold to this narrow view of who we want and "need" the other to be. When they don't meet our expectations, we think that we can't trust them. And in terms of their meeting our expectations, we can't.

It may be hard to accept this truth. Does it mean that we can never trust anyone? What kind of life is that? A life that's no longer a fantasy. Instead, it's a life based on the understanding that we can in fact trust everyone—trust them to be as they are. When we realize that we're living a substitute life, based primarily on the desire for comfort and protection, we can move away from our fantasy of trust toward a trust that's firmly rooted in the most basic practice stance: the willingness to just be with our life as it is. Whether or not we like it, whether or not it conforms to our wishes, is not the point.

The point is the simple willingness to just be with *whatever* arises—including mistrust, deception, and betrayal. The practice life is to see *all* of it as our path. Why would we want to do this? In order to allow *what is* to penetrate the layers of fear and protection that prevent us from living a genuine life of openness and connectedness. Using each arising instance of mistrust to break through our protected "self," we learn not to hold back our heart in fear.

Who do you think you trust? Do you trust your mate? Do you trust your teacher? What does "trust" mean? It usually means having an expectation that the other person will act in a particular way. What happens when this person doesn't meet your expectations, requirements, and projections? Are you hurt? Do you think, "I feel betrayed" or "This isn't safe"?

When we feel betrayed, we usually believe our thoughts and judgments. We believe them because we never even question the false grounds they're based on: our needs and expectations. Once we believe our thoughts, it takes all of two seconds to move into anger, blame, resentment.

In all of our relationships, we're looking for some guarantee of safety, some way to avoid being hurt. As soon as we do feel hurt—which is sure to happen eventually, given this requirement—it touches our core pain. Without fail, it reconfirms our deepest core beliefs: "I'll never be worthy," "They'll always leave," "I don't count," "I'll never be understood." At this point, we usually react with anger and resentment. Mistrust, at this level, is particularly hard to work with, because from an ordinary point of view our beliefs seem so justifiable. Any number of people would agree with us that someone else was to blame. Because it feels warranted, it's easy to forget that mistrust is really about *us*—not about what someone else did.

We need to see mistrust for what it really is. Fortunately, we have the infallible practice reminder that feeling hurt, mistrust, or betrayal is a sure sign that we're stuck in small mind's requirement that life should fit our fear-based pictures. When we have the good fortune to recognize this sign, we can then move from reaction and blame to the hard work of practice. We can see and label our believed thoughts, bring awareness to the physical experience of our emotional distress, and softly break through the layers of protectedness and armor by breathing the distress directly into the heartspace.

Practicing like this doesn't mean becoming a doormat and allowing others' unacceptable behavior to go unaddressed. We still have to be able to function in the real world, where there are concrete consequences for not keeping agreements or for acting in inappropriate ways. But even within that framework, regardless of whatever actions we might need to take, there is still the understanding that whenever there is reaction and defense, whenever there is hurt and blame, we must come back again and again to the basic question: *What is practice in this situation?*

Practicing in this way, we are less likely to believe in our self-righteous views of being betrayed—including the *believed* judgments of blame—and more capable of seeing through the "self" we take to be solid. Only by acknowledging and clarifying our habitual upside-down thinking, as well as opening to and experiencing the suffering that results from it, can we gradually move beyond our beliefs about trust, beyond our hurt and defense. This is how our substitute life is transformed into the more genuine life we all aspire to.

Even when we have a strong aspiration to awaken, it may be hard to practice with mistrust. The perception that we're being assaulted triggers our core fears, and the psyche mobilizes instantaneously to fend off the sense of groundlessness that these fears elicit. This is how we protect and defend our seemingly solid sense of "I." From a practice point of view, we need to open up to the fear and learn to reside in it. We also need to understand that sometimes we're not capable of doing that; the urge for safety is just too strong. We can't give up our sense of protection simply because we want to. We'll hold on to our protections and requirements until we no longer believe that we need them.

Sometimes we won't even be interested in working with a sense of betrayal. Then we need the willingness simply to attend to the fact that we don't want to practice with it. We can notice the extent to which we *want* to blame and to be right. We can notice how desperately we want to hold on to this secure sense of "me," no matter how miserably self-righteous it is. Perhaps we can at least avoid believing the usual self-judgments ("I'm weak," "I'll never be good at this," "I'm hopeless") and instead simply acknowledge them.

Ultimately, though, we need to understand that practice isn't about being safe, secure, or comfortable. It's not that we won't ever feel secure or comfortable; but the rock-bottom security that can come from many years of practice is a far cry from the security that we crave. We think we *need* to be able to trust, just as we think we *need* to be loved. But we have it backwards. As adults, we don't need to be loved. The only real emotional need, if we want to call it that, is *to* love. To love is our essence; it's who we are.

When we break through the layers of protectedness—of holding back, of shutting down, of demanding that life or a person be a certain way in order to give us what we think we need (whether admiration, safety, trust, or love)—what happens? We begin to touch the essence of who we are, which *is* connectedness and love. This is the only place where real trust can be found.

Whenever we have strong emotional reactions in real-life situations, practice is rarely clear and simple. Often, it's both confusing and difficult. Students frequently ask what they should do when strong mistrust arises in the middle of a conflict. They wonder if keeping their mouth shut and going off to meditate is really the best way to address what needs to be addressed. This question is understandable, because we fear being discounted. In general, however, it's almost always better to avoid getting hooked into self-justification and blaming, which is what inevitably happens when we open our mouths in the midst of a strong emotion.

In the midst of distress, what's important is staying with the feeling of groundlessness, breathing it into the heartspace, until we've worked with it enough to see ourselves clearly. Practice isn't about becoming a martyr or letting issues go unaddressed; certain things may, in time, need to be addressed. But it is *always* better if you can address them after you've seen through your own filters, expectations, and projections onto the other person. When you then go back to talk to this person, you'll be talking about your own reaction, instead of blaming them. And because they're not being attacked, it's possible that they'll also see and understand what happened more clearly.

Several years ago Elizabeth and I took a trip to Minnesota to watch Jenessa play in a college basketball tournament. I did something at the hotel that broke an agreement I forgot Elizabeth and I had made. Though it was in no way malicious, it triggered many of Elizabeth's deepest fear-based beliefs. Her reaction was immediate, and although she didn't attack or blame me, my *own* conditioning was triggered by the strength of her feelings. I found myself instantaneously caught in an intense reaction of fear and defense. There we were, in a hotel room in the middle of Minnesota, with the rug pulled out from under us.

Elizabeth and I normally have a harmonious relationship, and it was out of this that my sense of "trust" had solidified. Because we almost never fight, and because she had never done anything to hurt me, I felt a security, a "trust," that things would continue just the way I wanted. I was holding to the wishful thinking that I would never feel hurt in this relationship. But this seemingly small event had severely shaken my trust. At that moment both of us were living testaments to the tremendous power of the conditioning of core beliefs.

We were fortunate in that we both knew not to start blaming the other, even though it was difficult at times. We weren't suppressing; we were both working hard to really experience, on a bodily level, what we were intensely feeling. But it was difficult just to stay with the groundlessness, to not get lost in thinking, analyzing, self-justifying, and blaming. I kept breathing the difficult feelings into the center of the chest, where feelings can be most profoundly and genuinely experienced. In the middle of the day, needing a break from the intensity, I asked Elizabeth to go to the movies. Was this avoidance? Not exactly. Sometimes it's important to take a time out, to honestly acknowledge that you're at your edge. We went to the movies; and, later that day, although we were both still shaken, we had worked with our own reactions enough to see clearly what had actually transpired. Then we were able to come together with a deep and genuine sense of connection.

I had seen that I was holding a false sense of trust, based on the expectation that Elizabeth would continue to act in a particular way: namely, that she would never trigger my sense of hurt and defense. My idea of trust was rooted in the hope that she could protect me from my fears. But Elizabeth wasn't the cause of my fear that day, and to expect her to protect me from my fears was a misunderstanding of real trust. Dealing with our fears, which means being willing to let them in, is *our* job. When we demand that another person protect us in this way, which is the conventional notion of trust, we guarantee disappointment and suffering.

Seeing through my own notion of trust has been invaluable in terms of relating to others. In fact, this experience with Elizabeth turned out to be one of the best experiences we've had practicing together. In seeing through the illusion of trust, in being willing to experience the groundlessness that arises when this illusion is dispelled, in seeing that we don't have to protect and defend, in realizing that we don't have to hide our fears from each other—we experienced the genuine heart connection that's possible when we enter into the essence of who we really are, beyond protectedness.

I'm not saying that I no longer have expectations around trust. There will always be *some* expectations. But we can learn to see our expectations for what they are. When they aren't met and we experience disappointment, we must resist turning that disappointment back on another person or putting it back out in the world. Instead, we just need to realize what it is and work with it from there. That's when real healing can take place: when we break through the armor of fear. To come to know real trust means we've worked *experientially* through the layers of protection, need, and fear, and touched the bedrock of what's real. We've begun to understand that it's the willingness to just be with *whatever* arises that allows us to enter into Being itself, beyond any notions of trust or mistrust.

The most important thing to remember is that when issues of trust arise, we should first take another look at the situation. Remember to ask: Which pictures am I relating from? Remember to question the layer of perceived need that forms the basis of most so-called trust. We must see and experience our own need instead of blaming the person we think let us down. At some point, we might even thank the person for pulling the rug of security out from under us. In this way, disappointment can be our best teacher; it pushes us into fields where we would rarely venture on our own.

14
Forgiveness

WHAT DOES IT MEAN TO FORGIVE? Is there someone you don't want to forgive?

Forgiveness is often tainted with the idea that there should be some form of magnanimous acceptance of others even though they did us wrong. This understanding of forgiveness is *not* what a forgiveness practice is about. Forgiveness is about practicing with and healing resentment, the resentment that blocks our desire to live from our True Nature. Forgiveness is about loosening our hold on the one thing we most want to hold onto—the suffering of resentment.

In forgiveness practice, we work to see through our own emotional reactions. We practice noticing what stands in the way of real forgiveness. Genuine forgiveness entails experiencing our own pain and then the pain of the person to be forgiven. This experience can help dissolve the illusion of separation between ourselves and others.

Think of someone you feel anger, bitterness, or resentment toward: your mate, your parents (living or dead), one of your children, your teacher, your boss, a friend—anyone about whom there is active agitation in your heart. To make your understanding of forgiveness practice more experiential, keep this person in mind as you read this chapter.

When you bring this person to mind, how does it feel? Holding on to resentment often has the feeling of an unsettled account: "So-and-so has hurt me; therefore, they somehow owe me." As we cling to the hard, bitter feeling that someone owes us, we also may feel the need to pay this person back. As resentment festers, the attitude of "I'll show them!" takes over and hardens us. We shore up our hardened heart with the sense of false power and righteousness that arises with resentment.

If someone were to ask a spiritual teacher, "What should I do with all this resentment I feel against my friend?", the teacher might respond, "It's not good to hold on to resentment. Why don't you just let it go?" But *can* we just let it go? Even when we know how much resentment hurts us, we often don't have that option. If we could just let it go, we wouldn't be stuck in the throes of resentment. Letting go is not a real practice. It's a fantasy practice based on an ideal of how we'd like things to be.

Genuine forgiveness has three stages. The first is simply acknowledging how unwilling we are to forgive the other. We let ourselves experience the degree to which we prefer to hold on to our resentment, anger, and bitterness, even when we see how it closes us to living a genuine life. We see how we resist our inherent openness by choosing to stay stuck in our hardness. By bringing nonjudgmental awareness to how we resist forgiveness, we see clearly, not in order to feel guilty—which would be the result if we were living from the ideal that we *shouldn't* be resentful—but to enable us to experience resistance for what it is. We have to experience in our body how our unwillingness to forgive feels. We have to see our self-centered judgments clearly as thoughts, rather than accepting them as objective truths. Staying with the *physical experience* of resistance allows a sense of spaciousness to gradually develop, within which the tight fist of our resentment can be loosened. We can't move on to the second stage of forgiveness until we've entered into and experienced—in both our bodies and minds—the depth of our unwillingness to forgive.

The second stage is bringing awareness to the emotional reactivity toward the person we resent: to experience it without judgment, to see it with an open mind. As we visualize the person we resent, we notice what emotional reactions arise. We ask, "What *is* this?" Is it anger, resentment, bitterness, fear, grief? Whatever arises, we just experience it within our body. If we get lost in thoughts, memories, or justifications, we keep coming back to what we feel in the body. Where is the tightness, the contraction? What's the texture of the feeling? We stay with the awareness of our physical-emotional reactions as long as it takes to reside in them. That means relaxing into them, as painful as they are. At some point we no longer need to push them away.

Let's say we've been criticized repeatedly by someone. Instead of sulking or lashing back in reactivity, we remember the practice path. First we feel the anger and resentment rising. Next we listen to and label our thoughts: "Why do you always have to put me down?" "You're such a negative person." "No one should have to put up with this." Then we move from thinking and blaming into locating the resentment in our body. We feel the tightness in the mouth, the heaviness in the shoulders, the ache in the heart, the rigidity of the muscles. Staying with the physical experience, striving to avoid getting hooked into thoughts of self-justification and blame, we ask, "*What is this?*" We come back again and again to the physical reality of the moment. At this point we're not even entertaining thoughts of forgiveness; we're just bringing awareness to our suffering without trying to push it away. Once we can rest like this in our bodily experience, we're ready for the third stage.

The third stage of a forgiveness practice is to say words of forgiveness. It's important to realize that saying these words has nothing to do with condoning the actions of another. It's about forgiving the person, not what they did. It means seeing that the action came from the person's own pain. And the way we do this isn't by looking for the other's pain, but by attending to our own. Once we've attended to our own, we're more open to truly seeing the other's. At this point, saying words of forgiveness helps us open into the heart. Trying to open to the other's pain before passing through the first two stages of forgiveness practice—clearly seeing our resistance and resting in our experience of it—won't work; then we're just adding cosmetic mental constructs over our suppressed feelings.

Only after we've experienced how our own emotional reactivity stands in the way of real forgiveness can we truly understand that the other was just mechanically acting, in the only way a person can, out of beliefs and conditioning. We can then say the words:

I forgive you.
I forgive you for whatever you may have done
    from which I experienced pain.
I forgive you because I know
    that what you did came from your own pain.

In speaking of a poem he had written, the Vietnamese monk and Zen meditation teacher Thich Nhat Hanh recalled a letter about a twelve-year-old girl, one of thousands of Vietnamese boat people, who had thrown herself into the ocean after being raped by a sea pirate. This letter ignited so much rage in him that he wanted to get a gun and kill the pirate. At the same time he realized how easy it was to think only of the victim, not of the rapist. In no way was he condoning the sea pirate's act; he was pointing to the fact that when our hearts are closed, we're all capable of thinking, feeling, and doing horrible things. He called the poem "Please Call Me by My True Names," as a reminder that we must acknowledge *all* of our names, not just the ones we like to identify with. This is how we can access those closed-hearted parts of ourselves that we otherwise rarely encounter. In so doing, we can come closer to genuine compassion and forgiveness.

A few years ago I watched a TV documentary about the decision to drop the atomic bomb during World War II. My understanding had been that the decision was made to avoid losing over one hundred thousand men in a land invasion of Japan. Whether or not I agreed with this rationale, at least it had some merit. But the film pointed out that Japan had tried to surrender shortly before the bomb was dropped, approaching Russia as a third party to broker peace with the Allies. President Truman and his advisers decided not to negotiate, refusing even to hear the terms of surrender before they dropped the bomb. Dropping the bomb wasn't just about ending the war and saving American lives; it was also about showing Russia who carried the biggest stick. At that point in the program, I had such a strong reaction that I had to turn the television off. I felt tremendous self-righteous indignation against the people I had once believed were at least acting from some positive moral position.

In practicing with the rage—experiencing my own anger without the blaming thoughts—I remembered what Thich Nhat Hanh had said about his poem. I realized, *experientially*, that I was not so different from President Truman or his advisers. Nor was I different from those who dropped the bomb, or from the millions of people who cheered when they heard the news that a bomb was dropped on Japan. This was a sobering moment for me, considering that countless people were killed, and the suffering that was caused still reverberates. Whether or not the documentary had the facts straight, my self-righteous belief-based rage was as solid as a rock. In looking at my anger and opening to what had appeared to be so abhorrent, I saw that the fear-based, narrowly patriotic stance that had resulted in the death of so many wasn't really foreign to me at all. In fact, that conditioned trait was equally present in me.

This realization came from experiencing and seeing through my own anger. This is an important point. It's easy to comprehend intellectually that others are acting from their own protectedness and pain, and that we share with them certain traits that we prefer not to see in ourselves. But such conceptual understanding doesn't really touch our lives. It can never lead to the compassionate and genuine forgiveness that's possible once we've practiced with our own closed-heartedness and seen through it.

In practicing forgiveness, it is possible to move from living in our own isolated pain—which usually manifests as anger and resentment—to experiencing the universal pain that we all share. This suffering is what we realize experientially when we're able to see that we're not essentially different from those we've been quick to judge. Experiencing the truth of suffering frees us to move into the universal heart: the essential fact of our basic connectedness. In this place, the illusions that lead us to think we are separate and protected selves naturally dissolve. We no longer view the world through the lens of "us" versus "them." We no longer perceive the other as an enemy. We no longer seek revenge for what we regard as wrongdoing. We no longer demand recompense.

To enter into the process of forgiveness at this level, where the illusion of separation between self and other begins to dissolve, is a profoundly transformative practice. It's also challenging, partly because we don't want to do it, and partly because entering into our own pain is never easy. It is rare that the transformation of resentment occurs in just one or two sittings. If the resentment is deep, it may take months. Timing is also an important element. Sometimes the pain is too raw; we have to wait until the feelings are less intense.

It's sometimes said that you can't forgive others until you forgive yourself. While that sounds good, the formula is just a little too pat. It's a partial truth that misses the heart of the matter. What is this "self" that we must first forgive? There is no one solid self. This illusion of the self is the essence of the self-centered dream. Real forgiveness *is* our True Nature; it's not about one "self" forgiving another "self." This *experiential* understanding becomes apparent when we no longer believe in the illusion of the self. So instead of formulating notions of forgiving ourselves before or after forgiving others, we simply direct our healing awareness toward what *is*. We focus on wherever we feel resentment and whomever we can't forgive.

Even though it's some of the most important work we can do, forgiveness is one of the practices we least want to work with. The forgiveness meditation that follows this chapter is meant to be practiced over time, with patience. As we return to it regularly, warmth and compassion may gradually replace the hardness and bitterness of resentment. Remembering the words traditionally posted at the entrance of Zen temples can be helpful:

Let us be respectfully reminded:
Life and death are of supreme importance.
Time swiftly passes by
    and with it our only chance.
Each of us must aspire to awaken.
Be aware: Do not squander your life.

These words point to the folly of our upside-down way of thinking, of the magnitude of our constant decisions to let emotional reactions like resentment close us down. As we feel the pain of our hardness, and as the consequences of our unwillingness to open really hit us, perhaps we'll be more motivated to begin the essential work of forgiveness.

15
Forgiveness Meditation

WHEN ANGER AND RESENTMENT have calcified the heart, practicing forgiveness as a specific meditation can be very useful. This guided meditation directs awareness to areas that might otherwise go unaddressed. Its primary purpose is to help us see through the emotional reactions that stand in the way of real forgiveness. Essentially, it's about clarifying and healing our resentment. Real forgiveness requires first experiencing our own pain and then the pain of the person to be forgiven; from this understanding, the apparent barriers between ourselves and others can dissolve. The meditation has three parts.

In the first part, we *see* how unwilling we are to forgive the other person. We experience the degree to which we prefer holding on to our resentment.

In the second part, we bring into awareness all of the emotional reactivity we feel toward the person. The point is to *experience* it without judgment, to see it with "What *is* this?" mind. Only by clearing ourselves emotionally can we proceed to the third part.

In the third part, we "forgive" the other person. This is not the same as condoning their actions. It means that, through practicing with our own resentment, we come to *see* that the other person was simply acting from their own pain.

One of the most important aspects of this meditation is to bring awareness of the other person into the heartspace, the area in the center of the chest. Doing this may feel foreign and uncomfortable at first; this is a natural consequence of habit and resistance. Bringing awareness into the heart area makes it less likely that we'll spin off into simply thinking about our feelings. Rather, it allows us to experience them in a way that is both genuine and transformative.

Here are the instructions:

Sit or lie in a comfortable position, staying as still as possible. Take two or three deep breaths, then just breathe naturally.

Bring into awareness the particular person toward whom you feel resentment.

Feel for a moment what arises with even the thought of forgiveness. How much longer do you wish to keep your heart closed to this person, and consequently to life as a whole? If you had just a few days to live, would you want to continue feeling resentful and bitter?

Now remember the situation that sparked your resentful feelings. Feel whatever arises. Don't try to do anything; just experience the feeling in your body. Experience the degree to which you do not want to forgive this person. Experience the degree of unwillingness to even bring this person into your meditation. Acknowledge your unwillingness, and bring a nonjudgmental awareness to the sensations of resistance. How does it feel, in your body, to push the person away?

Allowing the resistance to just be, let the container of awareness widen around it. Now bring to awareness sensory phenomena from outside the body: hear the sounds, feel the air temperature. Feel how the texture of the resistance changes as a sense of spaciousness surrounds it.

Begin breathing into the heart area. Feel the texture of the heart.

Now try to bring awareness of this person closer to your being. Breathing into the heartspace, bring their presence, via the inbreath, into the heart. On the outbreath, just breathe out—not trying to do anything special. Without self-judgment, experience all of the arising emotions. Is there anger, resentment, bitterness? Is there fear or grief? Asking, "What *is* this?", notice whatever arises and experience it in the body. When you get lost in thoughts, memories, or justifications, come back via the breath into the heartspace, to the sensations in your body. Where do you feel tight, contracted, stiff? Where is the pain, the rigidity, the nervous quivering? How does it actually feel? Asking, "What *is* this?"—feel it. Stay with the awareness of your bodily-emotional reactions. Stay with them as long as is necessary to be able to reside in them, painful as they may be, without having to push them away. Stay here. Breathe. Hear the sounds outside. Hear the sounds in the room. Feel the air around you. Breathe. Reside here.

Return to your visualization of the person you wish to forgive. Draw this person's presence, via the inbreath, even deeper into the heartspace. As you feel the inbreath, say the person's name. Then say these words:

I forgive you.
I forgive you for whatever you may have done,
whether intentional or unintentional,
from which I experienced pain.

Whether it was from something you did
or from something you said, I forgive you.

I forgive you,
because I know that what you did
came from your own pain.

Repeat these words until you feel the barrier between you and the other person begin to dissolve.

If you still don't feel the sense of forgiveness, if some measure of hardness around the heart remains, just continue to breathe into the heartspace for a while, at least acknowledging the possibility of forgiveness at some future time. As you practice this meditation regularly, the process of forgiveness will gradually loosen the tight grip of resentment.

Having practiced this meditation a few times, it might be helpful to record it on tape, reading slowly and allowing two- or three-minute pauses to experience the arising feelings. Feel free to change the words to any that might resonate more naturally.

16

Opening into Loss

WE ALL CARRY WITH US accumulated grief—not just for people who have died, but for every situation that has ever brought about an intense emotional reaction to loss. Each time we feel loss—of a relationship, of our ideals and dreams, of our heroes, or of our faith—we're likely to bury the feelings and erect a layer of armor to protect us from feeling groundlessness, despair, and isolation. This is grief.

At some point, the path of practice brings us face to face with these layers of armoring that keep us constricted and protected in our narrow world. At the time we created these barriers, we might have needed them; perhaps we weren't yet ready to open up to the intensity of our feelings. Protecting ourselves like this can be a good thing. But if we wish to walk the path of awakening, relaxing into the spaciousness of gratitude and loving-kindness, we need to be able to open fully to loss. Opening into loss is one of the most difficult and also one of the most deeply fulfilling practices on the path.

Grief is difficult to feel because it's often both intense and elusive. It is constantly changing. Sometimes it manifests as anger, sometimes as fear, often as sadness and despair. Sometimes grief arises at what may seem the most unlikely times— when we hear a bird singing or see a flower in bloom. Within the sadness and tears, there often can be a deep, poignant sense of joy that doesn't make sense to us.

One small moment of grief often taps into the layers of un-resolved pain that we've been avoiding, such as fears of separa-tion, abandonment, and insecurity. Grief makes us feel heavy or weary, empty or incomplete, terrified, despairing, or ground-less. No wonder it often manifests as numbness that freezes out the feelings of separation, isolation, and loss of control. And always within grief and loss there is longing—for whole-ness, for completion, for harmony, for connection.

Many situations give rise to grief, not just the death of a loved one. Those who have experienced divorce have felt grief, as anger over the dissolution of ideals, or sadness at the loss of a sacred bond. Those who have lost faith in their religion, es-pecially after relying on it for support, may experience grief as emptiness and groundlessness. Anyone who has seen their he-roes or idols falter has experienced the feelings of sadness and incompleteness that are part of grief. When someone we love or admire dies, often our grief is more about ourselves than for the lost person; it is for our expectations and dreams that might never be fulfilled. And what about when our teachers, whom we have placed on a pedestal, show that they are all too human? Isn't the disappointment that we feel just another face of grief? Our anger, self-pity, and cynicism at such times are re-ally grief masking inner needs that may now never be met.

Often, when we are grieving for someone or something we have lost, we feel the pain and sadness of separation. We can feel it as an ache, as a tightness in the throat, as a hole in the center of the chest. Often fears are evoked—of isolation, of emptiness, of the unknown. And almost always there is the in-security of losing an anchor, the feeling of groundlessness that comes when we feel there is nothing to hold on to.

When the pain of loss arises, we have the choice to try to ward it off, bury it, or finally let it in. Considering the many faces of grief, it's no wonder that we so often choose to push it away. Not only is it difficult to make sense of loss, it's even more difficult to allow ourselves to feel the intense and often unpleasant sensations that follow. We often turn to culturally acceptable ways to avoid feeling the pain. Perhaps we adopt a feeling of martyred nobility in "my suffering." We might force ourselves to "be strong" or grieve "in the right way." Perhaps, as spiritual practitioners, we even try to assume the perspective of the Absolute, pretending to understand that "God works in mysterious ways," or that "life and death are one." But invoking these as *attitudes*, without having the corresponding inner understanding, or taking *any* position that prevents us from honestly facing what's really going on, is just another way of burying grief. It's one more way of armoring our heart against feeling fear and pain.

But exposure to loss, especially when it involves the death of someone we love, also has the power to awaken aspiration as few other circumstances can. Death, serious illness, or injury can jolt us straight into reality. Suddenly we see how much of our life is wasted on trivialities; we understand to what degree we're skating on thin ice; we appreciate that time is swiftly passing, and with it, our only chance of awakening to a genuine life.

Rethinking our priorities is the beginning of opening into loss. We're no longer so intent on clinging to our protections. We're no longer so interested in preserving comfort and safety as our gods. We begin to feel the pettiness of our attitudes and opinions. We begin to feel how strongly we hold our hearts back in fear. At this point, when our priorities have been turned right side up, we become more willing to allow the intensity of loss into our experience. But how can we do this? How can we best open into loss?

To open into loss is to open into the heart of experiencing. This involves bringing awareness into a point directly in the center of the chest, sometimes called the grief point. Acupuncturists classify it as the seventeenth point on the "conception vessel," a meridian, or line of energy, that bisects the front of the body. When we experience intense grief, this point is sometimes so sensitive that we can feel the tenderness when we press it with our fingers.

In this practice, we bring awareness first to the experience of loss as it manifests in the body. Perhaps we feel it as heaviness, as an ache, or as tightness in the throat. Breathing into the center of the chest, we take the sensations of loss directly into the heartspace. On the outbreath, we softly release. We're not trying to do anything with our experience of loss other than let it in. We're not trying to transform it. We're not trying to let it go. Rather, by breathing it into the heartspace, we're inviting ourselves to experience it in a new way, within the spaciousness of the heart, beyond thinking.

Recently two close friends were very ill with cancer. Anticipating that they would die soon, I was feeling sad and heavy. I wasn't even aware of how caught up I was in believed thoughts of doom, such as "Life is just too hard." But as soon as I remembered to begin breathing into the center of the chest, pulling the heaviness and the gloom directly into the heartspace, my experience of loss changed dramatically. Breathing into the heartspace undermined the force of the thoughts; and after only a few minutes of residing in the heart of the experience, my heaviness lifted. What remained was simply the sadness—but it was sadness without the heaviness, without the believed thoughts, without the melodrama. And within the sadness was also an openness to life and a profound sense of connection with my friends. It felt like a much more genuine and authentic response to the moment.

Some teachers say that feeling grief even as sadness is a sign of spiritual immaturity, that a truly awake being is free from all such reactivity. Would we feel grief if we had no expectations, no demands? Would we feel the pain of sadness if there were no dependency, no conditions?

This position, of course, is based on the point of view of the Absolute which says we are much more than just this body, this personal self. It emphasizes that only when we connect with the vastness of Being can we experience freedom from our normal conditioning, the conditioning out of which our grief arises.

Nonetheless, such glimpses into what is most real are not permanent. Even as we increasingly understand that our individual lives are fleeting, impermanent, and infinitely small within the immensity of the cosmos, we still will have our all-too-human feelings. Nor does a taste of the Vastness mean that our conditioning disappears. We remain human beings living in a conditioned world. This point is poignantly expressed in the Zen poem:

> Life is but a dewdrop
> Trembling on a leaf ...
> And yet ...
> And yet ...

We can only practice from where we are, namely the conditioned world. In this world we can't avoid grief and the pain of loss. What we *can* avoid is indulging in them. Through learning to breathe the pain directly into the heartspace—where me-based thoughts of self-pity, anger, and fear dissolve—we can move toward genuine contact with the inherent spaciousness of our True Nature. In practicing with loss, it's possible to work very specifically, step by step, with the conditions and attachments that intensify our emotional reactions. In fact, there's a very useful meditation practice that helps bring clarity to the process of grief even when there are no external catastrophes. I learned a version of this practice when I was training to be a hospice volunteer. I found it so powerful that I've continued doing it in a modified form ever since.

On twenty small cards I write the name of someone I am very close to, or one of my closely held identities (teacher, writer, etc.), or one of my favorite activities (nature walking, athletics, etc.), or some other important aspect of my life (good health, material security, etc.). These are my strongest attachments and therefore the places where my expectations and emotional loads are heaviest. Every couple of weeks I sit or lie down with the twenty cards in my hands. With my eyes closed I shuffle them while I begin breathing into the heartspace.

When I feel settled, I thumb through the cards until my fingers come to rest on a specific one. I ask myself, "What would it be like if I were to never have this in my life again?" Opening my eyes and reading the card, I try to feel what it would be like to experience the loss. At the same time, I stay aware of breathing in and out of the heartspace.

When it's a person's name on the card, I make a real effort to imagine that the person is dead. I imagine not being able to ever see or talk to the person again. I picture the specific situations in which I currently have contact with the person, and imagine the same situations without their presence. In short, I try to make this exercise as real as possible in order to actually feel the pain of loss.

Why would anyone want to engage in such a seemingly morose preoccupation with personal suffering? While it's true that this exercise can bring up some intense and unpleasant feelings, its purpose is not to perpetuate suffering, but quite the opposite. It allows us to clearly see and experience the roots of much of our pain: our expectations, our requirements, our attachments, and our cherished opinions. In exploring these roots, in experiencing the conditions out of which most of our suffering arises, we can gradually become more free of them. And unlike a real-life situation, where the shock of loss can overwhelm our ability to deal with it, this exercise is done within the more controlled environment of meditation.

What do we learn from an exercise like this? Imagining that someone we love has died, it's possible to clearly see how unimportant most of our agendas are. It's possible to *experience* the physical-emotional tensions that arise out of these agendas, thus clearing the way to a deeper appreciation of and connection to our life. Or in imagining the loss of material security, we can actually see and experience our clinging to money and possessions, freeing ourselves from at least some of the fears that so limit us. Practicing with our clinging can slowly free us of the emotional elements that *we ourselves have added*, those that block deepened connection and genuine appreciation. This anticipatory loss exercise is a small way to help lighten the burden of our unresolved pain. However, if you really want to really know the value of this exercise, you'll need to do it yourself at least a few times.

In my experience, there's no predictable or consistent response when focusing on a card. Sometimes I feel very little, in which case I simply end the exercise. Once, when one of my daughters' names came up, my reaction was so strong that I told myself to just try to stay with the experience for one minute and come back to it later. Often, however, I get fresh insights into my attachments, insights that I wouldn't otherwise gain. By continuing to breathe the feeling of loss into the heartspace, I'm able to experience a sense of spaciousness out of which arises a deepened sense of appreciation.

When we're feeling the inner chaos of grief with the accompanying panic of groundlessness and separation, what does it take to let it in? Certainly not an act of will, of ego. Perhaps the only word that can describe the process of opening into loss is surrender. Although we can't force ourselves to surrender, what we *can* do is bring awareness to the physical reality of the present moment. By bringing awareness to the center of the chest, by breathing the physical-emotional sensations of loss directly into the heartspace on the inbreath, we can experience the healing power of the spaciousness of the heart. Practice at this level is essentially a religious practice, because we're surrendering to something bigger than "me." We're entering the reality of "Thy will be done," where "me"—that struggling, separate self—can die into the spaciousness of the present moment. By opening into loss, by surrendering to the moment, by learning to reside in the unhealed pain we formerly pushed away, we slowly learn to live from the Heart that knows only connectedness.

17

Practicing with Sexuality

A YOUNG ZEN STUDENT realized he had some sexual difficulties. He thought about going to his teacher for help but felt a lot of hesitation: "Maybe it's not appropriate to talk to my teacher about sex. What's he going to think of me?" He went to the teacher anyway and described the situation. The teacher told him, "We must struggle with desire. We must *struggle* with desire. Go back to your cushion and learn what it means to struggle with desire."

The dutiful and persevering student went back to his cushion and struggled and struggled with his desire. But for some reason he didn't get very far. In fact, it seemed like his problem became even worse. So he decided to go to another teacher. This time he went to a teacher who was very famous for his deep Zen wisdom. He told the teacher about his situation. The teacher peered at him in an inscrutable Zen way and said, "No sex. No *not*-sex. Not one. Not two." And he rang his bell, dismissing the student.

The student was impressed by this teaching, but when he got back to his cushion, he had no idea what to do with it. Finally he decided to go to another teacher, one famous for his ardent devotion to practice. The student went to the teacher and described his problem. The teacher said, "Okay, this is what you need to do. Whenever your sexual difficulty arises in your mind, you just stop whatever you're doing and do one hundred and eight full prostrations, thinking only of Avalokiteshvara, the bodhisattva of compassion." The student really liked this advice, because now he had something he could do, something that he saw as being right in the heart of practice.

The student followed the third teacher's advice and became very, very good at bowing. But after some time, he felt as though he were squeezing a balloon right in the middle: as the middle would scrunch up, both ends were close to bursting at the seams. He realized he still wasn't addressing the situation.

Even though the student was discouraged, he decided to go to yet another teacher. He saw that maybe he was trying too hard, pushing too hard; so he decided to see a teacher who was famous for being laid back. He went to this teacher and described his situation. The teacher said, "No problem. Just be one with it. Just let it go." At this point, the student was becoming cynical. He realized this advice was just words. But still, he had a real aspiration to deal with his situation. He didn't want to just sweep it under the carpet.

Again, he found a new teacher. And finally, in this last teacher's reply, he understood what all the other teachers were telling him: "We don't talk about sex here."

Like most of the other "Zen stories" in this book, this didn't actually happen. I made it up to help us understand our own situation. It's true: we *don't* talk about sex, at least in terms of practice—especially in public. Why not? Because even though sexual themes, as well as so-called sexual freedom, are running through the mainstream of our culture, as a society we still regard sexuality as something dark and forbidden. Though we may not be conscious of this shadowy undercurrent, it's deeply embedded in our cellular memory.

As practitioners, the first thing we need to do is bring sexuality issues into our awareness. This is how we make them part of our practice world. We need to see our *own* expectations in this area. Because they may be hidden, they're often not what we think they are. For example, we may have been raised in a family where sex was rarely talked about or where there was little physical affection. Yet sexual freedom might have been very much the norm on television, in the movies, and among our friends. Although we speak the words of sexual freedom, and even act with apparent freedom, underneath it all we may still experience sex in terms of guilt and shame, or perhaps from a slightly prudish point of view.

Isn't sex one area of our life that goes mostly uninspected, at least in terms of practice? We have to look into the beliefs and attitudes that we haven't questioned, the ones we blindly accept as truth. What do we require of our partner? Do we know what these requirements are? Do we assume that our partner should respond whenever we want them to—that their role is to satisfy us? Do we have the belief that our partner should always ask before they touch? Do we believe that too much sex is unreasonable? Or do we have the attitude that not enough sex is unreasonable? Do we have the view that if our partner is not satisfied in the sexual relationship it means that somehow we're defective or deficient? If we experience this feeling of deficiency, what do we do? Do we try harder, lash out, close down, or even avoid sex altogether? Whatever we do, can we see it as just our conditioned pattern, our long-standing mechanical reaction?

Notice how you feel right now. How are you responding to these questions? It's possible to not even *want* to consider them in terms of practice. Yet sexuality is often a place where we don't know what we really think or feel. In just such a place—untouched by awareness—we're most likely to be caught right in the middle of the self-centered dream. As a result, we may find ourselves engaging in power struggles in the sexual arena that actually have very little to do with sex itself, but rather with control, guilt, or other issues.

For example, a student recently came to me to discuss what might be called a sexual problem. As we talked, it became apparent that the student's real problem was that he was experiencing his sexual behavior mainly in terms of guilt and shame, with the result that he withdrew from relationships, or at least from the physical intimacy in a relationship. When it became clear that this was not a *sexual* problem, but a problem related to believed thoughts, then he could practice with the distressing emotions in the same way that we practice with any emotion-based thought. But because he'd never applied the practice perspective to this particular area, he was calling his amorphous confusion a "sexual problem."

Along with opening our awareness to sexual issues, we also need to see where our deeply held beliefs are based in fear. Once we recognize our fears, we need to find where our workable edge is. For example, do we believe that we require monogamy in a relationship? That is, do we believe that our partner *has* to be sexually faithful to us? If this is our belief, is it based on a clear understanding of human nature? Or is it based on fear of being betrayed, abandoned, or seen as inadequate? Even if it's based on fear and insecurity, we may still need to acknowledge that this is our personal edge, beyond which we presently believe we cannot go. This is just where we're at right now. With such awareness, at least we're not basing our requirement of monogamy on simple or absolute moral terms. We're seeing it for what it is, as fear-based conditioning—not as some truth about reality.

Let's look at the flip side of this same issue. Perhaps we believe that monogamy is just an unnatural social constraint on our natural desire to be sexual beings. Is this belief based on some clear understanding of human nature, or on our own self-centered pursuit of pleasure? Do we then justify this pursuit by saying that monogamy is unnatural, thereby taking license to do what we want? If we see clearly that it is based on our own self-centered desires, then how do we practice with that?

We also have to be able to acknowledge the power of sexual energy itself—not as something bad or good, but just for what it is. What *is* sexual energy? Do we think we know what it is? Can we even say what it is? Can we see how much secondhand knowledge about sexual energy we blindly accept as truth?

Further, can we see how strong a role sexual desire plays in our life, in spite of how spiritual we may think we are? Can we see how, when desire is particularly strong, it can have its own mind, totally superseding any intention to confine it? When strong sexual desire arises, do we see that we often have the belief that we *must* satisfy it? This belief feels so solid that we see it as unquestionable truth. If this type of belief is running us, at very least we need to see it clearly. How do we practice with our intense desire for pleasure, which we feel must be satisfied *now*?

Perhaps we believe that all we really need to do is sit in meditation to deal with our strong sexual desires. Will sitting in itself take care of our difficulties? If we think it will, how are we really addressing this issue as practice? Are we expecting some magical transformation?

Sexual desire isn't the only issue we need to consider. Because desire is what it appears to be, at least we can see it with some degree of clarity. Sexual fantasies are more complex. While they are sometimes based on sexual desire, they might also have their roots in some other form of neediness. Can we see to what extent our fantasy is just a form of mental comfort to fill the hole of longing, to subdue the anxious quiver of being?

As sexual fantasies arise, can we meet them with the question, "What's the practice here?" Are we even willing to practice in this area? From a practice standpoint, we have to see our fantasies for what they are. Most often they're a defensive cover, almost like sucking our thumb. We'll do anything to avoid experiencing the hole of painful longing and loneliness that lies beneath these juicy thoughts. We need to see how unwilling we are to give them up. The more clearly we see our attachment, the more workable our practice is.

We also need to look at sexual longings that are imbued with our own particular darkness, such as the need to conquer or the need to pursue what we see as forbidden. How do we bring our own shadow world of private demons and core fears into the context of awareness? What about sexual addictions, which, no matter how fervently we pursue them, never lead to real satisfaction? Within these shadowy realms, what is practice? When we're under their influence, do we ever think to ask this question?

Labeling our sexual energy and fantasies as thoughts *is* possible. Such a practice might look like this: "Having a believed thought that I *must* fulfill this sexual desire." "Having a believed thought that I *must* fantasize." Labeling sexual energy in this way helps take away the intense identification we have with our desire, allowing us to see it as just our mechanical response, our obsession, or our own naturally arising phenomenon. When we believe what the mind tells us—"This desire is me, I am this desire"—we remain in a closed state of mind, which usually leads to disappointment and suffering. Practicing with sexuality in the context of awareness, we can relate *to* the desire instead of relating *from* the desire; thus we become free from the feeling that we *are* the desire.

Much of the heaviness and guilt around sexual issues arise directly from believing self-imposed moral judgments. The judgmental mind is merciless. Statements like "This is who I am, and it's bad; I shouldn't be this way" add another layer to our suffering. Our incessant self-judgment is compounded by the fact that we think we should be able to stop our desires and fantasies. We think that once we decide to stop, we'll be able to follow up on our resolution. Even though we make a decision wholeheartedly with one part of our being, other parts of ourselves may not be quite on board. Which "I" makes the decision? Someone once said that God created man with a brain and a penis, and enough blood to run only one at a time. We never quite know which part will be in charge. Disappointment and the pain of mechanical behavior may be what it takes to finally awaken our sincere effort to stop hurting ourselves and others by acting blindly.

Suppressing desire, one of the main efforts of our religious and cultural morality, is not the answer. Trying to suppress desire rarely works. Suppressing desire usually gives it even more power. Renouncing the object of our desire as "bad" may result in temporary disengagement, but in the end it usually just makes our desire and attachment stronger.

There are no formulas for dealing with the issues around sex. In addition to the fact that we rarely attempt to look at these issues in awareness practice, each situation has its own layers of complexity. For example, suppose someone is feeling very strong physical desire for his mate, yet senses a definite lack of mutual interest. This person is now caught between the strong urge to satisfy an intense physical desire and the protective urge to withdraw in order to avoid being hurt. What is the practice?

Again, there is no formula. The crucial thing is to bring awareness to what's actually going on. Once the inner conflict is clearly seen, we can look more deeply. Do we really believe that we *have to* fulfill our desire, just because we feel it? For many of us, this is a blind spot that causes a great deal of unnecessary suffering. Further, are we willing to look at our hurt, at the real or imagined "rejection" from our partner? What pictures are we living from? Do we believe that our partner should always share and respond to our sexual interest? Seeing our beliefs clearly will allow us to experience the hurt directly for what it is: a protective response to defend the fragile image of our "self."

Whenever we feel angry or hurt, we can be fairly certain we're in this protective mode. We can also be sure that we're trying to avoid feeling our core fears, whether they're based on the belief that we're not enough, that we're not worthy of love, that we don't count—whatever our particular flavor is. Working with these core beliefs, which run our lives not only in the sexual arena, but in countless ways, is an integral part of our practice. Our core beliefs need to be seen for what they are: deeply held assumptions about reality that our particular life circumstances have conditioned us to accept as absolute truth. Once we see this, which is no easy matter, we can enter into the physical experience of hurt itself, allowing ourselves to reside in the sensory world without wallowing in believed thoughts. What does hurt actually feel like? What is its texture? Where do we feel it in the body? Without thinking or analyzing, but through experiencing the moment itself, can we answer the question: "What *is* this?"

What will come out of it? No one can say. But the fact is that experiential awareness heals. It may take years of work and many failures, but what other choice do we have? The sexual issue always comes back, at least in part, to the basic practice of coming to know ourselves and learning the willingness to be with whatever life presents.

Again, practicing with so-called sexual problems often has little to do with sex itself, but instead with the overall patterns we've brought into the relationship. Often our impulses are the product of our minds rather than the natural arising of sexual energy. Just look at our fantasies, our attraction to the forbidden, or the pernicious judging and evaluating of sexual performance. How often do we experience or appreciate sexuality apart from the filters of our thoughts and conditioning? The main questions we need to raise are: To what extent are we aware of our particular conditioning and mechanical behavior? How, if at all, does cultural morality influence and regulate our sexual lives? In what ways are we driven by thoughts, fears, and core beliefs?

Furthermore, we need to explore how our emotional reactions around sex are tainted with self-judgment. The practice stance has nothing to do with moralistic notions of right and wrong, good and bad. Even with the sticky issue of monogamy, I'm not suggesting there's a right or a wrong position, and certainly not that I know what's best. All I'm saying is that most judgment—both of self and other—arises as a result of uninspected, deeply conditioned beliefs.

When the issue of monogamy arises, can we look at it clearly, devoid of our conditioned beliefs? The reason we do this isn't to create a new "should," but rather to see clearly what we're doing with our life. Having had my own struggles and confusions with this subject over the years, I know it's

hard to bring it out from the shadowy world of conditioned beliefs and relentless self-judgment. But I also know that with a
combination of perseverance and kindness, it too is workable.

There's no point in continuing to do battle with ourselves,
because there's no enemy within. Striving to perfect ourselves
by making ourselves more moral, with all of the implied self-
judgment, isn't the issue. The motivation is not to change ourselves or others, but to aspire to a deepened awareness and a
more genuine way of living. As long as we're having a war between one part of ourselves and another, both parts lose. Softening our relentless tendency to judge requires that we first see
all of our conditional beliefs for what they are. They aren't the
truth. They're just beliefs, whether they take the form of moral
dictates, opinions, or self-judgments. When we see this clearly,
we can relate to sexual issues from a more open place. Without
this softening, this lightness of heart, practice may never move
out of the heaviness of "my suffering."

Until we bring this subject into our practice, looking with
honesty and precision at what we do, how we think, and what
we believe, we'll continue to hurt ourselves and others. Can
you see how you hurt yourself by holding on to your pictures
of what sex is "supposed" to be? Can you see how you hurt
others with these pictures, expectations, and demands? Can
you see how these beliefs, and the reactions that come from
them, get in the way of real intimacy?

When issues arise around sex, it makes all the difference if
we can accept that these issues *are* our path. They're not obstacles on the path, but the path itself. Until we understand
this point, sex will continue to have its way with us, either
overtly in our behavior, or covertly in all of its disguised but
potentially destructive forms.

The power of our sexual energy cannot be denied. But this energy is in itself neither good nor bad. As in everything, heaven
and hell are both right here, right now. The difference between
experiencing our sexuality as heaven or as hell is rooted in one
thing only, and that is the clarity of our awareness.

PART FOUR

Efforts

18

Freeway of Practice

AT TIMES PRACTICE can seem very confusing. Sitting on the meditation cushion, we may wonder, "What exactly *am* I doing here? Am I supposed to be staying with my breathing? What about labeling thoughts—how does that tie in? And what about just residing in the stillness? How do my emotions and beliefs fit in with all the other stuff? Where do I incorporate a forgiveness practice or a loving-kindness practice?"

If at any given moment someone were to tap you on the shoulder and ask you, "What is practice right now?" a good percentage of the time the honest answer would probably be, "I don't know." This confusion doesn't arise because there are a bunch of different practices to choose from, but because we don't understand that the path of practice is very wide. All these approaches are different aspects of the same practice.

A useful analogy is to see the path of practice as a freeway with several different lanes. All the lanes are going in the same direction, but we choose the lane we need depending on conditions. Let's call the first lane the concentration aspect of practice, such as following or counting the breath. Such a practice is often useful at the beginning of a sitting, to settle our speedy mind. The strength of this practice is that it narrows our range; it helps us develop focus and stability. But this strength is also its limitation. Practice isn't about shutting life out; it's about opening to life, letting life in. Nevertheless, this limited practice is sometimes necessary and useful.

As we settle down in our sitting, we can then move into the second lane, which could be called wide-open awareness. This practice is to hear our thoughts, experience our bodily sensations, and be aware of our perceptions of the environment. Here we might practice the dual awareness mentioned in chapter 2, where we bring around a third of our attention to the sensations of the breath and to the perceptions of sound. Within that framework of awareness, we acknowledge and experience all the other sensations and perceptions that arise. Then we gradually widen the container of awareness to include a sense of our own presence, our own Being. In this place, we become more still and allow our experience to just be.

Lane three is our emotional reactivity, based on believed thoughts. Unbeknownst to us, cars from lane three are often cutting us off in lane two. The reactivity creeps up on us so that we don't even know it's there. When we sense this fuzziness, we may wonder, "What's the practice here?" The practice in lane three is to work directly with our emotional reactivity. Through thought labeling, we see how our reactivity comes from our endlessly thwarted requirement that life be the way we want it to be. We then reside in the physical experience of distress, until after some time we may catch glimpses of the deeply conditioned beliefs that keep activating it. This isn't an intellectual exercise; we have to see and experience how these deep-seated core beliefs reside in the body itself. This is riding in lane three, the fast lane, the lane of transformation.

All of these lanes are interconnected. To ride in lane three—practicing with our thoughts and reactions—we need the wider container of awareness of the second lane. In the second lane, we can experience the stillness within which the energy of our emotions—the thoughts and sensations—can move across the screen of awareness without activating our blind belief in them.

To reside in the wide-open awareness of the second lane, we often need the focus and stability of the first lane. In addition we may have to clarify the deep-seated belief systems of lane three; otherwise, these would subtly or not so subtly cover the whole freeway with fog.

The practices of forgiveness and loving-kindness belong to the carpool lane, because they almost always require taking the ride of practice with another person. Even though this lane is a separate lane with its own particular rules of the road, all of the lanes are going in the same direction—toward waking up. They're all based in the physical reality of the present moment. The point is to take into account *where we are* as we try to see how to proceed most effectively.

Rarely does practice in a sitting period just flow smoothly along. Intelligent practice requires that we use the intellect to know how to practice. We have to use the discriminating mind to ask two questions: "What's going on right now?" and "What's practice in this situation?" Without such an approach, we'll just ride our own roller coaster—from being totally speedy, to focused, to calm and imperturbable, then back to square one, where we're knee-deep in all of our emotional stuff. And we'll continue to believe that each passing state is our only reality.

The practice path is very wide. It even includes our resistance, our constant effort to avoid the anxious quiver of being. We might envision resistance as the breakdown lane, where we're stuck or stranded on the shoulder of the road. But whatever arises, the practice path requires that we simply see what is going on and then ask ourselves, "What is practice right now?", remembering that resistance to practice leads in the same direction as the other lanes on the freeway, as long as we see it clearly. As we learn to practice in this way, clarity emerges from our initial floundering in confusion; we begin to become aware of how this freeway of practice is exactly that—the way to become free.

19
Alarm Clocks

NASRUDDIN IS A BELOVED CHARACTER in Sufi stories, portrayed as a beggar, a dumbo, and a wise man all in one. In one story, Nasruddin is frantically looking under a lamppost for something. One of his friends comes along and says, "Nasruddin, what are you doing?" Nasruddin replies, "I lost my key. I have to find my key." His friend says, "I'll help you look for it; where did you drop it?" Nasruddin answers, "Over there in the alley." His friend asks, "Then why are you looking for it under the lamppost?" Nasruddin answers, "The light is better here."

In trying to uncover how best to proceed in practice, we're often like Nasruddin, looking in the wrong place. Sometimes we're looking in the wrong place for something that isn't even there. We think there's some magic key, some experience that will make practice permanently clear, especially in the midst of everyday difficulties. But there is no magic key, nor do we need one. Unless we're brand-new students, we already know what we need to engage in practice.

When I first started practicing in the late 1960s, I didn't have a teacher, I wasn't part of a meditation group, and I didn't know anything about Zen or meditation. But I was very zealous and tried hard to discover for myself what practice was. My motivation was to become free of the fear-based suffering that was such a big part of my life. So I developed various practices, and did pretty well with them for a while. In those days I had a lot of goals: five-year plans and one-year plans and daily plans. My path to liberation was clearly laid out. As funny as it sounds to me now, my plan was to become completely free from fear in five years.

There would be weeks and months when I thought I was making real progress. Then I would run out of gas and see myself as an abject failure. I'd get up my zeal again, start over, and do really well for a while. Then I would "fail" again. After repeating this cycle a few times, I concluded that I didn't have the key to practice: I didn't know what practice was. So I decided to find a group and a teacher. It's not that I was on the wrong track without them, but what I was doing was very crude. In part, I was asking the wrong question, "Where is the key to practice?" as if there were one big experience that would make it all clear. The question that I wasn't asking was "What gets in the way of practice?"

Even in those early days, I knew enough about what to do; but I didn't see the things that got in the way of doing it. One thing is our fluctuating motivation to actually do the work of practice. I've often wondered what determines our degree of aspiration or desire to awaken. Why does one person seem to want to practice more than another? Why do we practice harder at one time than another?

No one really knows the answers to these questions; what determines our degree of willingness is still a mystery. But even given the inevitable ups and downs in our desire to awaken, there are other factors we can consider in answering the question, "What gets in the way of practice?" We know that, in part, our resistance comes from continuing to believe that our strategies will work. These strategies may include trying harder, withdrawing to feel safe, finding diversions to avoid feeling pain, or hiding out in an identity such as victimhood. We're acting on the mistaken, usually subterranean, belief that these strategies will get us what we think we want. While our strategies can help move us toward some goals quite successfully, they don't bring us ultimate or lasting satisfaction. Over time, as life pounds us, they gradually wear thin. Disappointment is often our best teacher, but it may take quite some time to learn its lessons. For example, we may continue using our conditioned strategies even while seeing their futility.

There's another important factor in our resistance that we often don't even consider: how mechanical our behavior can be. We're simply not aware. We get lost in virtually everything we do, in virtually every identity or self-image that we wear. We rarely act with conscious intention; we rarely know who we are or what we're doing, except in a narrow and self-conscious way. Can we recognize how pervasively this waking state of sleep is our normal mode of being?

The purpose of recognizing our lack of awareness isn't to make us feel bad, as though we were poor, miserable sinners. Nor does it change the view that we are complete and whole just as we are, and that the essential nature of our Being, running underneath all of our strategies and protections, is connectedness and love. This is simply one of the paradoxes of life. As one teacher put it, "Everything is a mess, but All Is Well." On one level, all *is* well, but in order to realize this *experientially*, we have to work first with the layers and layers of mechanical conditioning and narrow identifications that make up our everyday existence.

The question is how best to deal with this state of waking sleep. What gets in the way of cultivating wakefulness? We first have to see, within ourselves, the extent to which we are asleep. We have to see how we live a substitute life—blindly following our conditioned strategies, repeating the same patterned reactions in a predictably mechanical way, and using them to hide behind our many defenses.

Sometimes we have to be jolted out of our protective shell. It may be the repeating shocks of life disappointments that wake us up momentarily to what we cannot ordinarily see. Practice is about learning how to receive these shocks: the things we don't like, the person who criticizes us, the job that goes wrong, the mate who leaves us, the health that fails us— whatever shakes us up. Sometimes it takes a teacher to provide an additional shock, to enable us to see that *one thing* that we just cannot see ourselves, or to help us see where we're getting in our own way.

Being jarred awake from our daily waking sleep is no different from being awakened from our physical sleep in the night. How do we wake up from our nighttime sleep? We use alarm clocks to jar us into wakefulness. The shocks we receive from teachers, or from life's disappointments, are like alarm clocks in that they pull us out of sleep into reality.

But there's another kind of alarm clock, one that doesn't come either from life's lessons or from a teacher challenging us. This alarm clock is one that we ourselves set up specifically to counter the unrelenting force of our mechanical conditioning. We set it up to jar ourselves out of our self-centered dream. There are three distinct types of self-imposed alarm clocks.

The first type is called *pauses in time*. Pauses in time are prearranged signals that we use to wake us up, to bring us back to *just being here*. One of my own pauses in time is the telephone ringing. Whenever the phone rings, instead of picking it up right away, I always let it ring twice. Even though I might be feeling efficient, wanting to answer it right away to take care of business, I just sit there and feel the breath in my heartspace as it rings twice. I'm not trying to do anything in particular, like getting calm or centered. I'm just feeling the breath and the heart, and noticing where I am, being present to the moment. Then I pick up the phone. One virtue of this particular practice is that its occurrence is so unpredictable. Since we never know when the phone will ring, it catches us right in the middle of all our craziness.

Another example of an effective pause in time is when we stop for a traffic light. Sitting there in the car, we can use the light as a reminder to come back to reality, if only for a few moments. If we're feeling impatience about wanting to get somewhere, the point is not to take a breath and try to feel patient. The point is simply to attend to whatever it is that's there. We listen to the voice of impatience and feel its physical texture. We don't try to relax or let it go. Instead, we're waking up to the fact that we're asleep in that moment, and experiencing what that moment is. When we *try* to relax, let go, or think positive thoughts, we're often just adding a cosmetic overlay to the moment, not really bringing awareness to what it is.

It is important to notice that a particular pause in time that we establish can be very effective for a few weeks or months, but then we might tune it out altogether. A good example of this is a picture I put in my entry hall of a young girl ice skating. Her arms are stretched out as if she's flying, and her head is thrown back as if she doesn't have a care in the world. Right in front of her is a sign that says, "Beware, Thin Ice." I placed this picture right where I would pass by it every day; and for the first several weeks, it worked as the perfect alarm clock. I'd smile whenever I saw it, because it would remind me in a lighthearted way of how much time we spend skating on thin ice, sliding through life oblivious to what we eventually have to face. It's one of my favorite practice themes. Seeing the picture would wake me up to the moment, providing that pause in time where I could just experience being present. Sometime later, I realized that I hadn't looked at the picture for weeks. Even though I'd probably walked by it several hundred times, I hadn't seen it at all!

As we begin to see this happen with practice alarm clocks, we see the power of the waking-sleep state. We learn that we have to counter this force by inventing new alarm clocks when the old ones no longer work. We change the picture, move it to another wall, turn it upside-down, or do whatever it takes for the alarm clock to do what it is intended to do: wake us up.

In my early years of practice, when I would "fail," say, by no longer seeing the picture, I'd condemn myself for being on the wrong track or for not being up for the task. At some point I finally understood that we can't wake up simply because we want to. We may wish with great fervor to awaken one moment, but our basic mechanicalness will predictably and inexorably arise to counter our aspiration. Thus we must invent one alarm clock after another, whatever it takes to awaken ourselves from the self-centered dream.

With pauses in time, we interrupt our conditional patterns wherever we can. For example, we could set our beeper watch to go off every thirty minutes. Whenever it rings, we check in with what's going on in that moment, simply *feeling* its texture. Other examples of everyday activities that can become pauses in time: reading aphorisms you've put on the mirror or in your wallet, turning your car on or off, opening your book to a bookmark with a practice reminder on it, sliding your credit card through the electronic scanner, or walking out to get your newspaper or mail. The possibilities are plentiful. The point is to just pause for a few moments and *simply be here*. The more of these small gestures you can insert into your day, the more awake and alive your day will be. You'll also become increasingly aware of just where and to what extent you are asleep.

The second type of alarm clock, one that I've been using for many years is the *practice menu*. To create a practice menu, assign yourself a different specific practice on each day of the week. Do the particular practice from the moment you wake up until you go to bed at night. Whenever possible, pick a practice that might be particularly appropriate for each given day. For example, since Monday is a day that normally triggers a higher level of irritation, I often choose it to practice the nonmanifestation of negative emotions. The practice is to not express negative emotions, inwardly or outwardly, for the entire day. The practice isn't meant as a moral dictate to suppress emotions. Its purpose is to bring awareness to the emotions as they arise; we make the choice not to fuel them, justify them, or solidify them by expressing them internally or externally. Being human, we'll no doubt express negative emotions at least on occasion when we're doing this practice. But, chances are, we'll express them less. More to the point, when we do express them, we'll become aware much more quickly of what we're doing.

Another example: if you are facing a day when anxiety or fear is likely to be triggered easily, you could practice saying yes to fear for the whole day. Whenever fear arises, instead of running away or trying to get rid of it, simply say, "yes." Invite it in and allow yourself to really experience what fear is. Notice what fear feels like. Notice where you feel it in your body and what strategies your mind uses to push the bodily discomfort out of your awareness.

Another menu practice that can help wake us from our mechanical patterns is called "It does." Instead of using the pronoun "I" when describing yourself, for one whole day substitute the word "it." This is particularly helpful when describing your emotional states. For example, instead of saying, "I'm irritable" or "I'm depressed," you say, "It's irritable" or "It's depressed." Just by using the different terminology, you can momentarily step outside of yourself enough to break the normally blind identification with your emotions.

Other items on a practice menu might include focusing the entire day on awareness of sounds, on the movement and stillness of the hands, or on feeling the breath rise and fall in the belly. You could also spend a day asking practice questions such as "Am I here?"; "What is practice right now?"; or "What is my life really about?"

You will remember to practice more on some days than others, but practicing even a few times a day is better than not doing it at all. Just deciding to follow a practice menu means you're making practice a central focus in your life. Both pauses in time and practice menus are reminders to return to reality. They can sharpen the fuzziness that we often feel in practicing with everyday life.

The practices on the menu aren't meant to add another "should" to your life. For example, to dedicate a day to the non-expression of negative emotions doesn't imply that negative emotions shouldn't arise; nor is it meant to propel us to sainthood via behavior modification. The point of these alarm clocks is to remind us to see clearly what we're doing. They're

ways to rouse ourselves from waking sleep and mechanical reactivity, and to enable us to see clearly what gets in the way of
awakening.

The third kind of alarm clock is the use of *tasks*. Tasks are
small efforts that take us against the grain of our mechanical
tendencies, particularly those toward comfort and protectedness. For example, we could specify a period of time to not read
while eating, to not eat sweets, or to not watch TV. We could
decide that we will talk to the person sitting next to us on the
plane, or that we definitely won't. We may decide to speak in
public, or to *not* speak in public. The task could be to refrain
from our normal people-pleasing behavior in specific situations, or to do something else that goes against our particular
self-image.

For example, suppose you get the urge to go dancing, but
you're not a very good dancer. There's no way you're going to
expose yourself as the physical klutz you consider yourself to
be. Because this situation takes you to your edge, it is a good
time to practice a task. The task isn't to become a good dancer,
although you might, but to expose yourself to one little place
where you're holding back in fear. It's about using the task as
an alarm clock to wake you from your conditioning and sleep,
to see them for what they are. In choosing to go against our
self-image, we have to be very clear that we're not trying to
change our behavior. We're not making a grim, determined effort to overcome our miserable self, to make ourselves into
that better person we'd love to be. The effort is much more
lighthearted, as is the attitude toward our sense of "self" and
our waking sleep. Thus we can maintain our resolve and our
seriousness of purpose without the task becoming a grim en-
deavor.

The purpose of a task is to push us to look at what we normally don't want to see. Tasks allow us to work, in small ways,
with our addictions and fears. We perform the task to experience the hole, the pain, and the fear out of which all of our addictive and protective patterns arise. Taking these small steps

at our edge, we keep our practice from becoming dry and stuck in seemingly comfortable routines.

Another twist on tasks is to enter new or foreign situations, not for diversion or pleasure, but to help ourselves awaken. Doing new things can awaken our senses, our awareness, and our sense of presence. I'm not necessarily talking about dangerous things, although tasks often seem dangerous, because they challenge our sense of routine and comfort. This sense of danger is part of what rouses us from waking sleep.

Recently I took up bicycling again after more than ten years. It's amazing how this little change brought me to experience the world with such freshness. This task didn't especially provoke my fears or challenge my defenses, but it did open me to something new. At present I'm doing one new little thing each week. I find that each small effort against the force of sleep and mechanical activity awakens a sense of vitality and presence.

Again, there is no one magic key that unlocks the secrets of practice. After all, practice—like the universe—isn't locked. There is nothing exotic or mysterious about what we need to do in order to awaken to reality. But there is one essential quality, without which practice can never really develop: perseverance. Perseverance keeps us practicing through the inevitable ups and downs of daily life. It allows us to keep going even when practice isn't pleasing in the ordinary sense. And one of the ways we make perseverance real is by using alarm clocks.

All the alarm clocks—pauses in time, practice menus, and tasks—serve to counteract the unrelenting, though sometimes subtle, force of our mechanical conditioning. We have to understand that we can't wake up simply because we want to. Alarm clocks give us ways to put our wish to wake up into action through specific efforts. If we don't do this, the result is predictable and verifiable: we'll simply stay asleep in our self-centered dream.

20

Be Kind

WHEN ASKED TO EXPLAIN the essence of his teaching, the Dalai Lama reportedly replied, "Be kind." This advice is so straightforward and simple that we can all relate to it. But in terms of our practice, what does it mean? If we take it to mean that we should *try* to act with kindness, isn't it just another moral dictate to change our behavior? Then wouldn't we be setting up just one more ideal of how we're supposed to be? How would that relate to the basic practice principle of being with our life as it is—not trying to change or improve ourselves? Yet, if we're not trying to change, does that mean that it's okay *not* to be kind—in fact, even to be unkind? These are important questions. Seeing what's at work in this area is key to understanding practice in everyday life.

Most of us are called to a spiritual discipline by the need to change our life. Certainly in the early part of our practice we all spend time *trying* to change. Our sense of dissatisfaction drives us toward fitting ourselves into whatever image we have of being more awake. We try to be more strong, calm, and clear, or less reactive, less negative. Yet, as we implement our strategies to fulfill our pictures of how we should be, we see that we can really do very little to change substantially. We make New Year's resolutions, we go on diets, we say we'll meditate every day, we try not to be defensive, we try to be nice and patient, but almost always we experience the disappointment and futility of this approach. Trying to change our behavior just doesn't seem to work, as the history of moralistic religion and the cultures associated with it have clearly demonstrated. Once we see this, disappointment rather than moral dictate becomes our best teacher. Instead of trying to change our behavior, we realize the sanity of learning to be with our life as it is.

But learning to be with life as it is doesn't mean acting however we want, manifesting anger and cruelty as we please. Genuine practice is always grounded in the aspiration to live from our True Nature. When practice comes from this aspiration, then, at the very least, we have a natural desire to try to avoid doing harm. But this is a subtle point, and can easily be confused with what we normally view as behavior modification.

The difference between the two is that when we aspire to allow our True Nature to reveal itself, the focus is on clearly seeing what impedes the process. For example, our hidden motives for extending kindness become clear—the expectation of acknowledgment, appreciation, and being seen as a better person. Further, we attend to all the ways we are *not* kind, such as manifesting cruelty and anger, or being controlling or petty. When we experience the ways we block our desire to live a genuine life of kindness and compassion, we *do* make an effort to change. But this effort comes not with the expectation that we'll stamp out our behavior. Nor are we making this effort to become a saint. Rather, the intention is to acknowledge and experience the anger and fear that underlie our unkindness. This effort means seeing and labeling our unkind thoughts, and residing in the direct physical experience—the "whatness"—in the body.

Curiously, it's the very expression of our anger and unkindness that prevents us from ever really residing in them. Why? Because the expression of negative emotions is almost always based on the erroneous assumption that someone or something outside ourselves is to blame for the anger or unkindness. To dwell in blame prevents us from looking at or truly experiencing our own negativity.

For example, suppose you're in a retreat sitting next to

someone who has a cold. At first you might feel sorry for her, even though you're relieved not to have the cold yourself. But as her sniffling and coughing continue, you notice your growing impatience. With each cough, you feel the heat run through you, "Why can't she be quiet? She should leave—her hacking's disrupting the sitting!" This can go on and on, blaming the other for your upset. After a while you might add a judgment: "I'm so impatient, so uncaring—what a failure!" Whenever we try to be virtuous—to fit some picture or ideal—we constantly come up against our own inner swamp. We then usually fall into blame, both of others and ourselves. Instead, we must learn to practice with our initial reaction. First we need to hear the thoughts; then we need to reside in the bodily experience of agitation and upset. This attention to our own reactions and experience is the beginning of being kind.

True human kindness comes forth when it will. Wanting to change is often the crux of the problem because it intensifies and solidifies what we're trying to fix. Yet a willingness to just be with what is—experiencing our unkindness without expressing or repressing it—*is* the solution. However, we can still try to act in a kind way, at least in order to avoid doing harm. And trying to be kind also highlights for ourselves how little natural kindness we manifest. We need to see and experience the depth of our unkindness in order for our natural human kindness to come forth.

If we look honestly at ourselves, we'll see the extent of our own "shit list"—all the people and things we feel unkindly toward. The practice is to observe all the ways in which we're unkind. First we simply see them for what they are—judgments and preferences. Then we practice residing in the particular physical experience—of agitation, of dis-ease—that arises when we require life to be a particular way. Paradoxically, the willingness to look at and attend to our unkindness is what ultimately heals it and transforms it into real kindness.

It's easy to be kind or patient when you're in a good mood or when things are going your way. But when things start to go in a direction you dislike, when life is not fitting your pictures, it's not so easy. The point is to see which particular pictures you're living from. For example, do you have the picture that you *should* be kind? Or friendly? Or loving?

As long as we are living out of pictures, or any kind of moral dictates, and as long as we have not yet addressed our unkind thoughts and impulses, we prevent ourselves from connecting with the basic human kindness that is the essence of our Being. But connecting with our natural Being—which is what all of us ultimately want—does not require that we stamp out our behavior and replace it with a new, improved version of ourselves. We just need to bring awareness to—*to see and experience*—all the layers of anger and fear under our unkindness. It is the seeing and experiencing that allow these layers to heal and transform on their own. It is through this gradual process that we can ultimately embody the deeper layers of kindness, of connectedness, of love, that are the essence of who we are.

21

Suffering and Joy

THE ARTIST PAUL KLEE wrote in 1905: "Imagine you are dead. After many years of exile, you are permitted to cast a single glance earthward. You see a lamppost and an old dog lifting his leg against it. You are so moved that you cannot help sobbing."

The depth of appreciation Klee expressed is truly akin to joy. It's the sort of feeling we can usually experience only after having learned from much suffering. The fifth-century Zen master Bodhidharma called this "bearing the unbearable"—seeing the unbounded wonder of life in the midst of death, suffering, and the utter aloneness of being human in a world of pain. We often hear this paradox expressed in pithy phrases such as "Every day is a good day" and "From suffering comes joy." Reconciling ourselves with this paradox is one of the essential streams of practice. But it's quite easy to distort this teaching in all sorts of subtle ways. What, really, is the relationship between suffering and joy?

To answer this question, we first have to understand what we mean by "suffering." Simply put, suffering is a wide range of emotional and physical reactions that result when we resist our life as it is. Holding to ideals of how our life ought to be, clinging to what we want, always leads to the same result: when our desires and expectations aren't met, we suffer. Whether it takes the form of anxiety, anger, depression, fear, or confusion, suffering is the direct consequence of wanting our life to be other than it is.

When any of these manifestations of suffering arise, our usual response is to try to get rid of it. We're even drawn to practice with the hope that it will save us. But we soon find out that practice is about learning to reside in our suffering, not about getting rid of it. Yet it's so easy to become confused and begin to distort this teaching.

What does it mean to reside in our suffering? Most generally, it means staying just where we don't want to be, experiencing in our cells the distress that arises when we hold to our requirements that life be other than it is. To simply reside in the physical experience of distress may sound simple enough. But this is just the point where most of our confusion begins, because we'll almost always add the subtle thought, "If I can just reside in my suffering, it will eventually disappear." In so doing, we're just adding another expectation to our picture of how our life is supposed to evolve. Even while residing in our suffering, we're resisting life as it is.

Another common distortion we add to practice is to invest our suffering with significance. We think our suffering makes us unique or somehow special; we see our plight as "deep" or "spiritual." Yet suffering simply presents us with a unique opportunity to learn; there's nothing inherently special about it. Taking a martyred view of suffering as special can keep us stuck in slimy virtue for our whole lives. In addition, we'll learn little from our suffering, because we're not open to it. Believing in our suffering or identifying with it keeps us from truly experiencing it and learning from it.

Another way we can distort the practice of residing in our suffering is by attempting to experience our distress with a forced detachment. This is just another protective strategy. The stiff upper lip, a stoicism bordering on forced cheerfulness, is a cover for trying to avoid suffering. It's just one more slimy virtue.

Another common confusion about residing in our suffering is the widespread belief that this practice is about "letting go." But is it possible to really let go of our deep-seated conditioned reactions to life? If we could, in fact, let go, wouldn't we all be feeling awake and joyful? Letting go is more a philosophy than an option. The real solution is not to let go of suffering but to let it *be* within the wider context of awareness.

This *willingness to just be* is the key to practicing with our suffering. It means seeing all the ways we confuse and distort the fact that we're in pain, and then ceasing to resist what is. We give up our one attempt after another to push our suffering away. Then the boundary between "me" and "the enemy—everything we'd prefer to avoid—begins to disappear. Finally we begin to feel joy, not as some bubbling Dionysian celebration, but as a quiet willingness to just be in the present moment.

Several years ago, in my role as a hospice volunteer, I met Robert, a forty-seven-year-old man who was dying of cancer with a variety of serious complications. When I saw him for the first time, he was lying asleep in his bed. His face was pale and gaunt, and he looked almost dead. Above the bed hung a large picture of him and his wife dancing on their wedding day. He looked so vibrant and happy in his white tuxedo, so very different from how he looked now.

When we met, I was at the beginning stage of what was to be an acute and prolonged relapse into an immune system disease I had had for some time. As a result, when Robert and I began to talk that first day, we connected deeply and immediately. Neither of us held back, neither of us was interested in the usual social pretensions, neither of us was trying to protect himself from the painful feelings that we were both experiencing. We were able to just meet and share our fears, but without the usual melodrama. We didn't talk about anything "spiritual"; he didn't have a concept about dying "consciously," and I didn't make any suggestions to him on how to practice with his difficult situation. His main concern was to make a video, a visual memento for his five-year-old daughter. But he was very weak and in considerable pain. On subsequent visits he mentioned that he was even considering suicide. He said he just wanted his suffering to end.

I visited him several times, for just a few hours, and we continued to have a strong and honest connection. Then, because my own health was rapidly declining, I couldn't visit anymore. Instead we spoke on the phone, continuing to share openly. As we talked about our common sense of grief and loss, I began to detect a shift in Robert. He no longer spoke of suicide. Even though his body was rapidly declining, we talked more about our connection; within our shared pain there was also a sense of shared heart. Within what appeared to be separate individual suffering, we found connectedness.

Robert knew that my immune system had been undermined by prolonged exposure to pesticides. One day he called to tell me about a remedy that might help me detoxify. Listening to him talk, I was thinking: "He's probably going to die any day now—why is he calling me to help with *my* difficulties?" His last word to me, which echoed in my mind as I put the phone down, was "Sayonara." When he died the next day, I wondered if he knew he was saying his final goodbye.

I found out later that he'd called a few people that day, trying to reach out, to give something back. That's what he chose to do on the last day of his life. Here was a person who had real difficulties, and he didn't want pain and suffering any more than the rest of us do. In fact, at one point, he was ready to end his life on his own. Yet something transformed. He willingly surrendered to his life as it was. He then experienced a grace made possible by learning to bear the unbearable. He learned to say yes to life and to give something back.

We may not be forced to face our suffering through circumstances as intense as Robert's, but all of us have our own measure of difficulty with which to practice. How willing we are to learn from our suffering will determine the quality of our life. How deeply we understand what it means to trust in, to reside in, *whatever* comes to us—especially the unpleasant and the unwanted—is the key to opening into genuine appreciation and joy. Yes, we will confuse this issue and distort the practice; yes, we will resist our lives in endless ways; but gradually, with perseverance, we will also begin to learn. We can't simply stop confusing, distorting, and resisting, but we can learn to see what we do. It's this seeing that allows us to gradually re-side directly in the bodily experience we call suffering. Only then can we understand that what we call joy is simply the willingness to be with what is—including, and especially, the suffering that none of us wants.

22

Humphrey Bogart on Practice

SEVERAL YEARS AGO I heard a story about an older man who in his early teens had lived in a home for juvenile offenders in northern California. What he remembered most about this home was visiting day. Every Sunday friends and relatives could come visit the boys. Every Sunday he would look out through a large knothole in the wooden fence to see who was coming, but nobody ever came to visit him. Reflecting back on this time of his life, all he could remember was the sadness, desolation, and loneliness that he felt when he was looking through that knothole.

As this young boy grew up, he led a very hard life. He entered into a life of crime and was in and out of jail. But in his middle years he began to learn from his difficulties and somehow turned his direction completely around. In his later years he went back to the boys' home to revisit the experiences of his youth. This time, when he went into the yard and looked through the hole in the fence, what he saw was the hillside with its rolling green grass and majestic old oak trees. Essentially, he saw the beauty of the world.

This story is a good reminder that when we're caught in our self-centered dream—wanting, needing, obsessing on our "self"—we're seeing things as *we* are, not as *they* are. We see them through our own hole in the fence, our filtered perceptions clouded by believed thoughts and emotional reactions. But as we follow the path of the genuine life, we begin to see reality more and more clearly. We begin to see things more as they really are, and with that clarity, a deepened appreciation frequently arises.

Living the genuine life requires us to keep coming back to the most basic questions in practice: What's the point? What are we really trying to do in practice? Are we working mainly to reduce our personal difficulties—to have nicer relationships, less confusion, less anxiety? Are we thinking we can fix ourselves up into a better self? Is it just some pretty and sophisticated form of therapy? We have to answer these questions honestly.

In doing so, we'll see that our motivations are often complex. They rarely address just one part of ourselves. Our aspiration to awaken to a more genuine life is almost always entwined with our desire to make our lives less difficult. As we observe this ambiguity, we sometimes react by judging one part as good and another as bad. Yet who's to say what's bad? If the mistaken belief that practice will solve our personal problems keeps us practicing, is that so bad? When our problems don't disappear, perhaps we'll feel disappointed enough to see that practice isn't what we hoped it would be. Maybe we'll have learned enough to be able to see more clearly what we're doing with our lives. Perhaps we'll be able to practice with one less filter of expectation. Maybe by learning what practice is *not*, we'll learn what practice *is*. Yet ultimately, in order to find the genuine satisfaction that we're looking for, our view of practice has to include more than our self-centered desires for a problem-free life.

Let's come at this from a different perspective. Recently I heard that on a clear night we can see, at best, about two thousand stars. But modern astronomy has discovered that in our galaxy alone there are four hundred billion stars! That's a big number to imagine. The real kicker is that our galaxy, with its four hundred billion stars, is only one of four hundred billion galaxies. I may be off by a few billion, but it's a pretty big picture nonetheless. What comes to mind are the words of Humphrey Bogart at the end of *Casablanca*: "It doesn't take much to see that [our] problems don't amount to a hill of beans in this crazy world."

What has this got to do with practice? In view of the immensity of the cosmos, should we not take our difficulties so seriously? But what about needing to attend to our difficulties, needing to experience our emotions, needing to be in our bodies? Do the discoveries of modern astronomy make a mockery of our efforts?

On one level, certainly not. When we're knee-deep in our private mess, we're rarely aware that we're even on a planet, let alone on one among billions. We can practice only from where we are, which always makes where we are the very best place to practice. This includes practicing with our messy lives, where we're so often caught in our incredibly limited self-centered dream. In fact, when we exclude what's going on at the moment and instead base our practice on trying to experience just the Vastness, we tend to create a lot of mayhem in our life, because we're ignoring our shadowy world of hidden agendas. We *do* need to work with our own hill of beans—our difficulties, our dramas, our limited views. And yes, we can only do this work through the body we have, since it's our only vehicle for sensing, feeling, and experiencing.

Nonetheless, on another level, it's essential that we bring the big picture to mind once in a while, if only to remind us of what we tend to forget. Unity consciousness, our basic connectedness, enlightenment—whatever we want to call it—isn't some "thing" that we either have or don't. It's not necessary to connect with the four hundred billion galaxies to step beyond our own boundary. We can realize our capacity for enlarged awareness in small doses—by experiencing the song of a bird, feeling a cool breeze on a warm day, looking into the eyes of a newborn baby, sharing the pain of another being. Every event of our daily life is an opportunity to connect with the vastness of Being.

Humphrey Bogart was making an important point. When we forget how small our drama is, we're likely to lose ourselves in a narrow view of practice—trying to change, trying to get, trying to do. Practice on this level often becomes all too serious. The point is not to ignore our stuff—disappointment is still the best teacher. But we don't have to get lost in our suffering. Working with it isn't the only way to wake up; life is too short to close the door on other possibilities. If we think we can't really open the door until we work with everything that gets in the way, we forget that we'll always be clearing the path, until we die.

When we find ourselves getting lost in our personal drama, grimly "doing our practice," or weighing ourselves down with a serious outlook, it might be good to remember Humphrey Bogart's words. That our little dramas don't amount to a hill of beans is not the voice of cynicism, but of lightening up. It reminds us that all that is required to appreciate the sunshine, the fresh air, or *whatever* is right in front of us, is the willingness to drop the harshness of our judgmental mind. When we can do this, we become open to the moment from a more spacious and kindhearted awareness.

Of course, we can also get lost in seeking special states of mind, in trying to have some big experience that will magically transform our lives. But this grasping for "enlightenment" is very different from just being open. Just being open is the continuous soft effort to simply be here, which always entails enlarging our container of awareness to take in more than our narrow world of self-centered perceptions. As the container enlarges, so does the sense of spaciousness, appreciation, and heartfelt connectedness that is the nature of our Being. Tasting the essence of each moment teaches us that yes, we *are* this body, but at the same time, we are much, much more. And the essence of the moment is as available from changing a hose in the garden or walking down a busy street in the middle of the city as it is from gazing at the stars or sitting in meditation for a week.

In a way, we get good at what we practice, and what we've been practicing our whole lives is making a big drama out of a little hill of beans. Now we have the opportunity to practice something else: working with that drama when necessary, to be sure, but not just getting lost in that aspect of practice. Instead, we can cultivate a curiosity for the unknown, stay open to tasting the vastness, and not lose sight of the bigger picture. What is the bigger picture? It's looking through the knothole of a fence without the filter of our conditioned judgments, being able to see what's there—the wonder of the world.

In Zen we hear about a little bird sitting on our shoulder who asks, "Is today the day you're going to die?" This is not a somber bird, nor is it asking the question in a dramatic way. Ever so lightly, it's telling us that living the genuine life is about *living*. It's reminding us to be kind in our practice, to be kind in our life. In these moments the Unconditioned aspect of Being can naturally flow through this conditioned body, without being impeded by the grimness of our incessantly judgmental mind. This bird is giving us a message we need to hear over and over again: "Time is fleeting. Don't hold back. Appreciate this precious life."